THE CURIOUS
WORLD
of BUGS

DANIEL MARLOS

THE CURIOUS
WORLD
of BUGS

The Bugman's Guide
to the Mysterious and
Remarkable Lives
of Things That Crawl

A PERIGEE BOOK

A PERIGEE BOOK
Published by the Penguin Group
Penguin Group (USA) Inc.
375 Hudson Street, New York, New York 10014, USA
Penguin Group (Canada), 90 Eglinton Avenue East, Suite 700, Toronto, Ontario M4P 2Y3, Canada
(a division of Pearson Penguin Canada Inc.)
Penguin Books Ltd., 80 Strand, London WC2R 0RL, England
Penguin Group Ireland, 25 St. Stephen's Green, Dublin 2, Ireland (a division of Penguin Books Ltd.)
Penguin Group (Australia), 250 Camberwell Road, Camberwell, Victoria 3124, Australia
(a division of Pearson Australia Group Pty. Ltd.)
Penguin Books India Pvt. Ltd., 11 Community Centre, Panchsheel Park, New Delhi—110 017, India
Penguin Group (NZ), 67 Apollo Drive, Rosedale, North Shore 0632, New Zealand
(a division of Pearson New Zealand Ltd.)
Penguin Books (South Africa) (Pty.) Ltd., 24 Sturdee Avenue, Rosebank, Johannesburg 2196,
South Africa
Penguin Books Ltd., Registered Offices: 80 Strand, London WC2R 0RL, England

While the author has made every effort to provide accurate telephone numbers and Internet addresses at the time of publication, neither the publisher nor the author assumes any responsibility for errors, or for changes that occur after publication. Further, the publisher does not have any control over and does not assume any responsibility for author or third-party websites or their content.

First edition: October 2010

Library of Congress Cataloging-in-Publication Data

Marlos, Daniel.
  The curious world of bugs : the bugman's guide to the mysterious and remarkable lives of things that crawl /
Daniel Marlos.
    p. cm.
  Includes bibliographical references and index.
  ISBN 978-0-399-53613-7
  1. Insects. 2. Arthropoda. I. Title.
  QL467.M345 2010
  595.7—dc22   2010017791

PRINTED IN THE UNITED STATES OF AMERICA

10 9 8 7 6 5 4 3 2 1

*This book is dedicated to my mother, Pearl Marlos,
who nurtured my early interest in nature with her own love for gardening
and then indulged me by regularly taking trips "to the country"
along the Pennsylvania–Ohio border, where I could tramp about in the
woods and fields and explore the creeks in search of bugs.*

Acknowledgments

A very special thanks to my longtime collaborator Lisa Anne Auerbach, whose zine *American Homebody* launched the "What's That Bug?" column.

I am indebted to Eric Eaton, whose frequent contributions and difficult identifications helped give the website credibility.

Without Daniel Jacobs's generous gift of bandwidth, What's That Bug? would not have had the continuous web presence that it has enjoyed for the past several years.

And finally, thank you to the web-browsing readership, whose dedication and contributions of entertaining stories and wonderful photographs have created a true network of bug enthusiasts.

Contents

Introduction

XI

Introduction

W HEN I STARTED working on the idea to write a curious
miscellany of wacky, wonderful, and intriguing facts about bugs
that I've collected during my years of research, I knew I had a cast of over
1 million characters worldwide, including 86,346 recorded insects in the
United States and Canada alone. Each one had a story I could tell. There
were more species than the number of words I needed to write the book.
How was I going to whittle down the cast to just include the stars?

I decided to start with the top ten most common requests that are
emailed to WhatsThatBug.com, including the potato bug with its
strangely humanoid appearance, the house centipede that often
startles folks watching television when it scampers across the carpet,
and the western conifer seed bug that just wants to come in out of the
cold so it can survive through the harsh winter.

I would also have to include benign insects with such frightening
appearances that they often become unnecessary carnage, like the
harmless male dobsonfly with his grotesquely disproportional
mandibles. Other scary bugs are actually beneficial because they prey
on potentially harmful species, like the dragonfly, which feeds on
mosquitoes yet has the misfortune of being associated with the devil
in countless languages. Then there's the petite pseudoscorpion,
which enjoys ridding your home of flies and other unwanted
intruders, and the giant water bug, which is also called an electric
light bug because it is attracted to porch lights.

I couldn't forget the insects found in remote locations that have such interesting life cycles that an anthropomorphization could easily become the basis of a cinematic melodrama: The Apollo butterfly, which is found in the alpine regions of the Northern Hemisphere, and the rain beetle, whose range is limited to the forests of the Pacific coast of North America, are in that category. You'll read about how the male Apollo butterfly ensures that his mate remains faithful, and about how a flightless female rain beetle lures her mate to her bedchamber.

When I began writing the insect identification column "What's That Bug?" in my longtime collaborator Lisa Anne Auerbach's fledgling photocopied zine *American Homebody* in 1998, I had no idea that a column about an all but forgotten childhood interest would spark such a nostalgic curiosity in me. When the column went online two years later, I realized that the tagline mantra I had been reciting ("everybody wants to know what's that bug") proved to be more prescient than even I had imagined. The Internet opened up a whole new readership, and under the guise of the Bugman, I proceeded to respond to the web-browsing public's letters and photographs, attempting to identify the curiosities encountered in the home, lurking on the tomato plants, or spotted while on vacation in Costa Rica.

Through the years, patterns began to emerge among the letters. At the end of each year when identification requests from the Northern Hemisphere are sparse, photos of cicadas with crazy names, brightly colored spider wasps dragging around enormous spiders to feed their brood, and Christmas beetles with perfect holiday timing pour in from Australia. Like clockwork, in the late winter, the first luna moth sightings occur in the southernmost portions of the range in Texas, Florida, and Georgia. That first encounter a lucky observer has with the graceful and ethereal luna moth is an unforgettable event, and the feelings of awe are inevitably communicated in the identification requests I receive. Each year as I post images of the first luna moth, I lament that to this day I have never witnessed a living specimen of this glorious insect in the wild despite all the childhood hours I spent waiting in the backyard with the porch light turned on or gazing up at streetlights in wooded areas. The luna moth has always been my insect holy grail, and I still haven't given up hope that I will eventually see one in the flesh, or more correctly, in the exoskeleton. Each summer when I return to Ohio, a bit of the child returns as I scout likely illuminated habitats near woodlands for this evasive creature of the night.

Though the luna moth has always proven elusive for me, I do have many fond memories of insect encounters, and I hope this book will spark a similar interest and curiosity in you. Each spring, I would don the galoshes and wade into the vernal pond that formed across the highway to observe the intricate web of life. Fairy shrimp abounded and were preyed on by predatory aquatic naiads of dragonflies and damselflies, and fierce water tigers would patrol the still waters, devouring tadpoles and any other available victims. In the autumn, when the goldenrod and milkweed towered over me in vacant lots, huge preying mantises would wait patiently on the blossoms, feeding on the grasshoppers, wasps, and butterflies that were attracted to the blooms while enormous orb weaver spiders waited patiently in the centers of their webs for hapless creatures to become hopelessly ensnared. Perhaps the pangs of loss I felt at habitat destruction when new homes and businesses replaced my cherished open spaces contributed to my current activism to preserve the vanishing California Black Walnut woodlands in Los Angeles.

So, gentle reader, turn the page and prepare to enter the fascinating and curious world of bugs.

DANIEL MARLOS

1

ENTOMOLOGY AND ETYMOLOGY

What's in a Name?

T HE SIMILARITY BETWEEN the words *entomology*, "the study of insects," and *etymology*, "the study of words," is interesting, as is the manner in which insect names are selected. Scientists use a rigid binomial system based on genus and species to ensure that worldwide, regardless of the language spoken, the same insect will have the same name universally. Common names, however, are often colloquialisms or local names for bugs that are quite colorful and descriptive but with a limited range of use. They do not translate from language to language, and there's sometimes a great deal of overlap; the same common name can be used for diversely different species.

Anytime a new creature is discovered, it is given a ponderous, tongue-twisting, scientific, two-part name that corresponds to the genus and species. This system of identifying and naming life-forms was created by Carl Linnaeus a couple hundred years ago, and it is now used by the scientific community to identify all living things. The genus names generally come from descriptive root words derived from ancient Greek and Latin, and occasionally the species names do, too, though as often as not the species name refers to the person who discovered it, some other individual, or even the location of the discovery. While the scientific names are the surest way to properly refer to a specific species, that system is generally overkill when one is making small talk at the dinner table or breaking the ice at a party.

Because scientific names are so difficult to pronounce, they're rarely used by the average person who still needs to call the crawling or flying creature in question by something, hence the need for colorful colloquial names. Common names for some insects are very location specific, and sometimes numerous species are described by the same name. They're also specific to one language and are often based on local lore, superstition, or even outrageous fantasy.

The term *bug* really needs to be defined before we go any further. Entomologically, true bugs are insects that belong to the suborder Heteroptera of the order Hemiptera. True bugs have an incomplete metamorphosis and sucking mouthparts. *Insects* can be distinguished from other *arthropods* by the way their bodies appear to be cut up into three parts: head, thorax, and abdomen. They also have three pairs of jointed legs, a pair of antennae, and a pair of

compound eyes. Insects may have one or two pairs of wings or none at all. So entomologically, all bugs are insects, but not all insects are bugs. In the language of the layperson, the term *bug* has been broadened to include all insects plus any other creeping or crawling invertebrate. That definition has allowed WhatsThatBug.com to respond to questions about spiders, centipedes, scorpions, snails, and slugs as well as insects. I'll exercise the same flexibility here, though most of the bugs you'll read about truly are insects, but not necessarily true bugs.

This chapter delves into the science of insect identification and offers playful information about how insects are named. It is often the goal of an entomologist or naturalist to discover a new species that will provide a legacy for the discoverer's name. Fifty years after his death, the accomplished author Vladimir Nabokov had his status as an amateur lepidopterist cemented in the annals of history when his name and some of his best remembered literary characters'

names were used to identify newly discovered butterfly species in South America. Nabokov examined museum specimens of butterflies and theoretically devised a radical new taxonomy for their classification. Though Nabokov published his findings, the results were not accepted by the scientists until lepidopterist Kurt Johnson led a team to the Andes to discover new species and to prove Nabokov's theories. Many of the newly discovered species were named after famous and infamous Nabakovian characters like Lolita, Humbert Humbert, and Charlotte Haze, all from the controversial 1958 novel *Lolita*, a fitting tribute to an author who loved to invent new words. The account of the Latin American expedition and discoveries is chronicled in the 1999 nonfiction book *Nabokov's Blues* by Kurt Johnson and Steve Coates.

· *The Outline of Animal Taxonomy* ·

KINGDOM
    PHYLUM
        CLASS
            ORDER
                FAMILY
                    GENUS
                        SPECIES

In addition to these seven major categories, subcategories and supercategories are sometimes created. The term *tribe* is occasionally inserted below the subfamily level and before the genus level. Sometimes in this book, I will speak about a unique species, but in most cases, I will try to speak more generally. There are over 3,000 species of mayflies worldwide, representing over 400 genera and at least 42 families, but their characteristics are universal. The mayflies of North America act like the mayflies in Europe and the mayflies in Australia.

• *The Classification of a House Fly* •

Using the accepted outline of animal taxonomy, this example will show how the common house fly is classified and how it receives its scientific name.

KINGDOM: Animalia
  PHYLUM: Arthropoda
    SUBPHYLUM: Hexapoda (six-legged arthropods)
      CLASS: Insecta
        SUBCLASS: Pterygota (winged insects)
          ORDER: Diptera (true flies)
            FAMILY: Muscidae
              SUBFAMILY: Muscinae
                TRIBE: Muscini
                  GENUS: *Musca*
                    SPECIES: *domestica*

SPRINGTAILS: CLASS COLLEMBOLA

Springtails are primitive, minute, flightless insects that often gather in great numbers garnering attention through numbers, not size. Recent taxonomic changes have removed them from the class Insecta and placed them in their own class. The largest springtails are a mere ¼ inch in length. Many species have a tail-like appendage known as a furcula, which snaps against the ground, springing the insect into the air in a hopping motion, hence the common name springtail. In their natural state, springtails are usually found in damp locations like leaf litter and in areas with decaying organic matter. Home gardeners are likely to encounter springtails in

their compost pile, hopping about whenever the surface layer is disturbed. It is estimated that there are more than 300 species of springtails in North America alone, and assuredly many more yet undiscovered species worldwide. According to the Discover Life website (www .discoverlife.org), over 6,000 species of springtails have been identified worldwide, and they literally are found worldwide, ranging even to frozen Antarctica and the surface of the ocean. By conservative estimates, there may be as many as 250 million individual springtails per acre, making them the most abundant arthropod on the face of the planet. Because they feed on decaying organic matter, springtails play an important role in keeping the planet healthy by assisting in the creation of fertile soil by the

production of humus (the natural compost that is created when organic material becomes part of stable soil).

MAYFLIES: ORDER EPHEMEROPTERA

The order name Ephemeroptera has Greek roots for "wing" and "living for a day." The common name *mayfly* would imply that these creatures make an appearance in the month of May and at no other time of the year, yet nothing could be further from the truth. In actuality, mayflies may fly at any month of the year, depending on the species and the climate, but their numbers are often the greatest in

The Greek word *ephemeros*, which means "lasting but a day," forms the root for the name of the order, and truly most mayflies live but a single day. If conditions are right, they may live a few days, but shortly after becoming winged adults, most mayflies mate and die. Fly-fishing fans are quite familiar with mayflies, and many fishing flies and lures are patterned after mayflies. Flies patterned after adults are known as spinners, and flies tied to resemble the subadults are known as duns.

May. In many temperate climates, including the Great Lakes region near Lake Erie, the population of mayflies reaches astronomical proportions in May each year. Then, mayflies appear in gigantic swarms and the air is thick with their fluttering forms. Pavement under lights that attract them can become slippery with their trampled and smashed bodies, but this swarming behavior is critical to the survival of many fish and birds that feed on the bounty of the swarm.

Mayflies do not feed as adults and possess atrophied mouth-parts that are useless for feeding.

DRAGONFLIES AND DAMSELFLIES: ORDER ODONATA

The origin of the order name Odonata refers to "tooth," and the fact that the insects represented here have strong

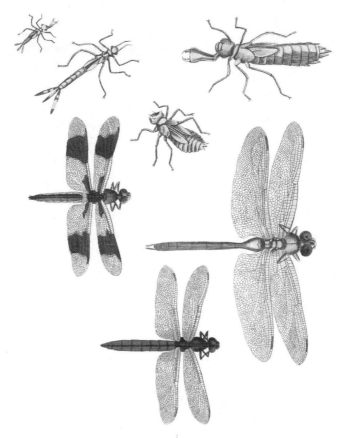

teeth on their mandibles. Dragonflies and damselflies are predatory, primitive, winged insects that are generally found in proximity to bodies of water. The immature forms are aquatic and are often called naiads, being named after the mythological Greek nymphs that were associated with bodies of freshwater. It isn't too difficult to imagine that dragonflies were named after flying dragons because of their large size, but modern dragonflies are nowhere near as large as their ancestral predecessors. Fossilized dragonflies that became extinct at the time of the dinosaurs had a wingspan as large as 30 inches

across; the largest modern dragonflies from South America, however, measure in at a much more modest 7 inches. Though they look similar to dragonflies, damselflies are generally smaller and more delicate, and they are weaker fliers. There are so many legends associating dragons with damsels that it is not too far of a stretch to imagine the weaker branch of the insect order to be given a name that relates to the ancient tales, and I take creative license with that suggestion.

Thirteen Maleficent Names (and Three More for Good Luck) for Dragonflies

Though dragonflies are beneficial predators, their large size, frightening appearance, and aerodynamic flight is responsible for a wealth of myths from around the world. There is a great deal of overlap in these myths, which consistently relate

dragonflies to the devil, horses, snakes, and sewing. All of these beliefs can be found throughout the United States, probably due to the immigration of individuals from other lands where the myths originated. In some cultures, notably Japan, the dragonfly is viewed as an omen of good luck, but alas, most of the myths are positively diabolical. It is important to note that these are colloquial phrases that often have limited geographic distributions, but human migration often carries the terminology far from its place of origin. Myths and superstitions are passed from generation to generation, so many of these colorful names are still in use.

Devil's darning needle: based on the folk belief from the northeast portion of the United States that the dragonfly would sew up the lips of children who asked too many

questions or, alternately, of children who lied, women who scolded, and men who cursed. The darning occurred while the guilty parties slept.

Ear sewer: based on the folk belief from the San Francisco area that dragonflies will sew up a person's ears.

Ear cutter: probably the origin of the previous name and attributed to England. One might imagine that the ear cutter is the evil version; the ear sewer might then stitch up the damage in the manner of a surgeon.

Water witch: a translation from the German *Wasserhexe*, which on the surface might seem evil, but it could equally refer to dowsing or water witching, a process by which water can be located using a forked twig. Perhaps thirsty travelers followed dragonflies to quench their thirsts.

Snake doctor and snake feeder: names based on a folk belief from the American South (snake doctor), and a slight variation from the Midwest (snake feeder), that dragonflies take care of snakes and can even bring snakes back to life.

Adder's servant: based on a Welsh belief that dragonflies are in league with snakes. This term is especially maleficent since the term *adder* refers to any poisonous snake.

Blind stinger: translated from Swedish *Blindsticka* and referring to the belief that dragonflies could pick out a person's eyes.

Eye poker: translated from Norwegian *Øyenstikke* and similarly referring to the belief that dragonflies could pick out a person's eyes.

Devil's little horse: translated from the Spanish phrase *caballito del diablo* and based on the belief that the devil could ride about on dragonflies.

Evil old hag's horse: based on a Lithuanian myth that witches rode about on dragonflies.

Horse stinger: based on an Australian belief that dragonflies swarmed around horses that were jumping about and kicking as if they were being stung. The horses probably were being stung, but by biting flies and not the dragonflies, which were most likely feeding on the biting flies.

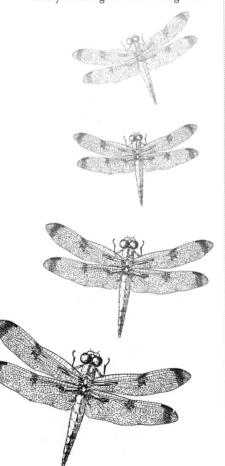

Hobgoblin fly: based on a Swedish superstition that hobgoblins and other woodland spirits used dragonflies as twisting tools of trickery and treachery to bend the minds of humans to immoral and devious ways.

Troll's spindle: translated from the Swedish *trollslända* and based on the superstition that trolls used dragonflies as spindles when weaving their clothing, but the trolls could also use them to poke out their enemies' eyes.

Halloween pennant: an orange and brown North American species, *Celithemis eponina*, that gets its common name from arguably the most pagan and frightening of all holidays.

Widow skimmer: a North American dragonfly, *Libellula luctusa*, with a species name translating to "mournful" or "sorrowful," referring to the wings, which appear to be draped in mourning crepe.

Dragonhunter: a large North American species, *Hagenius brevistylus*, that preys on other dragonflies, hence its common name.

EARWIGS:
ORDER DERMAPTERA

Skin and wing, a reference to the leathery texture of the wings, provided the Greek meaning for the order Dermaptera. Just the name *earwig* conjures up an image that is probably not too far-fetched from this dangerous-looking, but harmless insect with forceps at the tip of its abdomen. Earwigs are also called pincher bugs, though the nip of the forceps is perfectly harmless. The common name *earwig* is thought to originate from an Anglo-Saxon word *earwicga*, which, according to Charles Hogue, the curator of the entomology collection of the Natural History Museum of Los Angeles County from 1962 until his death in 1992, translates to "ear beetle" or "ear worm." Earwigs are generally nocturnal creatures that hide during the day

among debris, under rocks, and in snug crevices. Earwigs feed on plants, organic matter, and small insects.

Though they are not theoretically considered garden pests, more than one rose fancier has strolled the garden in the morning only to discover that the first opening buds of a prize rose have become both food and home to one or more earwigs. The common name probably originates from a time when medieval Europeans lived in stone and sod houses without much insulation. Mattresses were often made of straw, which provides both a food source and a habitat for the earwigs. It is not at all unlikely to imagine an earwig seeking shelter in the dawning light by crawling into a person's ear, only to have that person awake in alarm yelling *"Earwicga!"*

GRASSHOPPERS, CRICKETS, AND RELATIVES: ORDER ORTHOPTERA

The name for the order Orthoptera was derived from two Greek words meaning "straight" and "wing." This order contains a vast number of the insect world's music makers, though they do not use their mouths to produce sounds. Sound is produced by rubbing body parts together, generally the legs, a technique known as stridulation. The order is divided into two suborders, separating the members with long antennae from those with short antennae. The orthopterans with short antennae are the grasshoppers in the suborder Caelifera, and it isn't too difficult to explain that common name if anyone has ever walked through a field and startled a long-legged grasshopper into

hopping away and hiding in the grass. The orthopterans with long antennae, in the suborder Ensifera known as long-horned orthopterans, include insects like crickets and katydids, both of which are common names derived from onomatopoeic renderings for the sounds made by the insects when calling for their mates.

The Curious Potato Bug

The potato bug, which is one of the most frequently made identification requests on WhatsThatBug.com, is quite the curiosity. Potato bugs, long-horned orthopterans in the family Stenopelmatidae and natives of the western portion of North and Central America, have numerous other interesting common names that do not make much sense. Despite living underground, potato bugs do not prefer to eat potatoes. Though they are also called Jerusalem crickets, they did not originate in Jerusalem. Other names are much more descriptive, including children of the earth from the Spanish

• A Trio of Insect Musicians •

THERMOMETER CRICKET

The snowy tree cricket is also called a thermometer cricket because the temperature of the surrounding air can be calculated by the frequency of the chirps in the insect's mating call. Counting the number of chirps in 13 (or according to some sources 15) seconds and adding 40 will give the temperature in degrees Fahrenheit. Snowy tree crickets are found across North America from coast to coast.

KATYDIDS AND THEIR SONGS

Charles Hogue poses this interesting explanation for the name *katydid* in his landmark book *Insects of the Los Angeles Basin*. Katydids got their name because of a legend involving a homely maiden named Kate and her comely unnamed rival for a young lad's affections. When the lad fell in love with the more attractive maiden and scorned Kate's affections, he mysteriously died. The townspeople all questioned, "Did or didn't the proud Kate do him in?" The katydid was the only witness who was able to provide testimony each summer night by proclaiming "Katy did."

CRICKETS AND GOOD LUCK

In China, crickets are kept in cages for good luck. If found in the house, many cultures tolerate their presence, and their songs are said to bring blessings to all who are fortunate enough to hear them. My own first tiny cottage in Los Angeles had a large black field cricket that lived in the bathroom sink

drain, and it would sing throughout the night. Care needed to be taken to run the water slowly in the sink so as not to wash the cricket into the sewer. The cricket lived there for many months.

niñas de la tierra, due to the almost human appearance of the insect's head, and skull insect from the Navajo name, also a reference to the insect's head. It is interesting that the closest relatives to potato bugs are the wetas of Australia, New Zealand, and South Africa. These insects have a wealth of legends associated with them as well.

PREYING (PRAYING) MANTIS: ORDER MANTODEA

Because of their large size, predatory habits, and numerous humanlike qualities, preying mantises are familiar even to small children. *Mantis* means prophet, or seer, in Greek, so the correlation to religion is not

a modern notion when it comes
to the spelling variation praying
mantis, the name that is most
commonly used. The Greeks
observed the connection
between the hands of a prophet
while in praying mode to the
stance of the praying mantis's
upraised front legs while
awaiting prey. Some writers,
including me, prefer the secular
verb *preying*, as it more correctly
describes the intent of the pose
of the preying mantis while
attempting to capture food.
Some other common names for
this bug are kneeler, soothsayer,
devil's horse (not to be confused
with the dragonfly), rearhorse,
and mule killer (not to be
confused with the velvet ant
known as the cow killer).

COCKROACHES: ORDER BLATTODEA

Cockroaches are a group of
primitive insects with a rich
fossil record. The largest
fossil cockroach was found in
a coal mine in Ohio and it
dates to 300 million years ago.
Other than being larger than
most modern cock-
roaches, there are only
insignificantly different
details between the
fossilized specimens and
those living today.
This lends credence
to the popular

conception that long after humans are gone from earth, the planet will be ruled by insects, with the amazingly resilient cockroach as the most likely survivor. Unlike many of the other etymological explanations of name origins, the cockroach probably received its English name because of the auditory similarity to the Spanish name *cucaracha*. The English words *cock* and *roach*, a bird and a fish, were probably combined without any concern for the meaning, but strictly because of the similarity of the sounds. Though there are several species of cockroach that infest human domiciles, the vast majority of the more than 3,500 species worldwide are benign insects that inhabit woods and jungles and would not be found reproducing inside the home.

WALKINGSTICKS: ORDER PHASMATODEA

The Greek word *phasm*, meaning "phantom or apparition," is an apt root for this order of well-camouflaged insects. The common name *walkingstick* obviously refers to the fact that these insects appear to be sticks until they begin slowly walking, revealing their presence in the greenery. Walkingsticks are a primarily tropical order of insects, but they are represented by at least 29 North American species. A recently discovered species from Borneo, *Phobaeticus chani*, is nearly 2 feet long. One southern species is the twostriped walkingstick or musk mare. The name *musk mare* originates because of two unusual characteristics of this species. The first is that adults are almost inevitably discovered in the act of mating, and the smaller male is found riding on the back of the female, attributing to her the characteristics of a mare. The musk is undoubtedly a reference to a chemical spray that the

musk mare can expel with surprising accuracy, often finding its mark in the eyes of a potential predator. Some sources say that the chemical is capable of causing temporary blindness and, in extreme cases, corneal damage.

TRUE BUGS AND RELATIVES: ORDER HEMIPTERA

This complex and diverse order is characterized by incomplete metamorphosis and mouthparts that pierce and suck fluids from either plants or animals. While there are some important predators in the order, there are also many devastating agricultural pests, including aphids and scale insects. Often mistaken for beetles, the soft-bodied true bugs including stink bugs are also placed in this order.

A Closer Look at Selected Hemipteran Families

Shield bugs got their common name because of their body shape. They're also called parent bugs because of their maternal care to eggs and young.

Giant water bugs, also called toe-biters because of the painful bite they can give to swimmers, and electric light bugs because they are attracted to lights, are among the largest flying insects in North America. They are also

one of our most frequently asked identification requests at WhatsThatBug.com, where images of them arrive nearly every week. Giant water bugs, which at up to 4 inches in length are the largest true bugs in the world, are eaten in Thailand.

Bed bugs get their common name from their habit of entering beds at night to suck blood from those in dreamland. These nightmarish insects hide under the mattress or behind pictures and wall hangings during the day.

Leaffooted bugs are also called big-legged bugs and, in certain tropical species, flag-footed bugs.

All these names are references to the greatly enlarged tibia on the hind leg of many species.

Water striders are sometimes called water spiders because of their spiderlike appearance. They stride across the water surface on four outstretched legs with amazing speed and accuracy. Though their legs form slight dimples on the surface of the water, the body weight is dispersed in such a manner that they are able to move about without piercing the membrane of the water's surface.

Stink bugs earn their popular name because many members of the family are capable of producing odors from glands. The odors are used as a means of self-defense. Stink bugs are not the only insects capable of producing musty odors, but they have earned the distinction of getting the name. One of the more familiar stink bugs is the harlequin bug, *Murgantia histrionica*. Harlequin bugs get their name from their gaudy colors of black, red, yellow, and white and the intricate pattern of their markings. In all, there is a strong resemblance to a harlequin's colorful wardrobe. Gardeners who plant vegetables in the cabbage family are probably familiar with this bright garden pest.

Unlike the stink bugs, the scentless plant bugs do not possess scent glands and do not release an unpleasant odor when disturbed. It is curious that this lack of an attribute has resulted in a popularly used common name.

Assassin bugs are predatory insects with formidable hunting skills that duplicate the stealth skills of an assassin. Assassin bugs feed on other insects, sucking the body fluids out with their piercing mouthparts. These piercing mouthparts are fully capable of biting humans, and several species are known to have a significantly painful bite. One of the largest and most unusual species is the wheel bug,

Arilus cristatus. The wheel bug gets its common name from a coglike projection on the back of the mature insect. Contributors to WhatsThatBug.com have referred to the wheel bug as prehistoric looking, and it has been called a stegosaurus bug on more than one occasion.

Spittlebugs get their common name because of the immature nymphs' habit of creating a nest that resembles foamy spittle. The spittlebug produces this spittle as a fluid voided from the anus that is combined with a mucilaginous substance excreted by glands in the epidermis. Immature spittlebugs rarely leave their nest of spittle that can be found on the stems of the plants, often weeds, on which the nymph is feeding. Adult spittlebugs resemble leafhoppers.

Ant cows are a common name for aphids, which are among the most destructive agricultural insects both on a commercial scale and in home gardens. There are over 1,300 species of aphids recorded from North America alone. Aphids suck the juices from plants, often causing the new growth to wither. They reproduce at an alarming rate, and the new buds from a prized rosebush can quickly be covered with hundreds of aphids during an infestation. Aphids secrete a sweet, sticky substance from the anus known as honeydew, and this honeydew is most attractive to many species of ants. The ants stroke the aphids to encourage them to produce honeydew, and the ants will also protect the aphids from enemies and move them from location to location where the aphids can find a fresh source of food. This symbiotic relationship between the ants and the aphids has led to the common name of ant cows.

Peanut-headed lantern-flies are curious insects with several interesting common names. German artist, naturalist, and pioneering feminist Maria Sibylla Merian painted the peanut-headed lanternfly, *Fulgora laternaria*, at the turn of the 18th century while in

· 17–Year Locusts ·

North America is the home of one of the most unusual insect phenomena on the planet, the periodic appearance every 17 years of enormous swarms of cicadas known erroneously as 17-year locusts. Locusts are a completely different order of insects, but because of the great numbers of the periodical cicadas, the misnomer has been appropriated.

The periodical cicadas belong to the genus *Magicicada*, and though a given generation emerges every 17 years (every 13 years in the southern part of the range), there are broods in different parts of the country that are on different cycles. In any given year, in some place in eastern North America, in the late spring and early summer when the temperature of the ground has warmed sufficiently, great numbers of periodical cicadas will emerge and create an ear-splitting buzz for several weeks. They provide a necessary fatty food source for numerous birds and mammals. At the end of their adult life, they will die, and in 17 years, their progeny will appear on schedule.

Twelve broods of 17-year locusts have been identified, and an additional three broods of 13-year locusts are known from the southern portion of the range. Brood X, probably the best known of the broods, last appeared in 2004 and is due again in 2021. Brood X has one of the greatest ranges, including Delaware, Georgia, Illinois, Indiana, Kentucky, Maryland, Michigan, New Jersey, New York, North Carolina, Ohio, Pennsylvania, Tennessee, Virginia, and West Virginia.

Surinam to observe and draw living Amazonian insects. She erroneously reported that the large head of this insect, which resembles a peanut, was capable of glowing in the dark. A few years later when Carl Linnaeus began the daunting taxonomic task of using his binomial system to name every known living creature, he accepted Merian's observations and named the species *F. laternaria*, leading to the English name lanternfly. Though insects in this group do not emit light, the name has stuck, and in many circles the myth of luminosity persists. It is interesting that in parts of South America, including Ecuador, Colombia, and Venezuela, this insect is called the *machaca*, and it is believed that if a person is bitten by it, he or she must have sex within 24 hours or die. Since the peanut-headed lanternfly is incapable of biting, the belief is probably nothing more than a means of urging a reluctant paramour to surrender through fear and coercion. This same insect is also sometimes called an alligator bug because of its resemblance to that large reptile, which might be responsible for the belief that this harmless insect is capable of biting humans.

Cicadas are among the largest of the free-living hemipterans. In North America, a common cicada is known as the dogday harvestfly because it looks like a fly and appears each year during the dog days of summer, the hottest and most sultry days between July and early September in the Northern Hemisphere.

AUSTRALIAN CICADAS HAVE THE BEST NAMES

Australians have a certain fondness for their cicadas that borders on mania. This has manifested itself in the colorful and creative common names for various species.

Green grocer, *Cyclochila australasiae*: This highly variable cicada has a different common name for each of its color variations, with green being the most common color morph. The green grocer is a reference to the vegetable venders of yore and might refer to the bright color of the insect, which is similar to the color of lightly blanched greens (as opposed to when they're overcooked).

Yellow Monday, *Cyclochila australasiae*: The relatively common yellow version of this species. It is rumored that the name was given by a child, perhaps because the insect was encountered on a Monday. The name was in common use by the end of the 19th century.

Chocolate soldier, *Cyclochila australasiae*: The relatively rare dark tan morph of the species is similar to the color of candy, though the origin of the reference to the military is unknown.

Blue moon, *Cyclochila australasiae*: Perhaps the rarest of the color morphs of the species is equated to the rarity of a blue moon, the second full moon in a calendar month, which occurs only in years with 13 moons. This is an annual cicada, meaning that individuals appear every year,

but it has a long period of development underground. The nymphs live under the surface, feeding on sap from roots for 7 years. This means that the genes responsible for the rarer color variations have become isolated to specific broods or populations.

Masked devil, *Cyclochila australasiae*: While the diabolical reference is undeserved, the mask in question is a black marking on the face of an orange-brown insect. This is a high-altitude color variation.

Cherrynose or whisky drinker, *Macrotristria angularis*: The dipsomaniac's signature red nose has contributed to the moniker for this loud species, perhaps an apt reference as a person is often prone to boisterous communication while in his cups.

Tiger prince, *Macrotristria godingi*: The yellow and black stripes of this cicada are its most prominent feature.

Typewriter, *Pauropsalta extrema*: It isn't difficult to imagine the staccato tapping on an electric typewriter when one hears this cicada sing.

Bagpipe cicada, *Lembeja paradoxa*: Just as the bagpipe is inflated with air while being played, the male bagpipe cicada is capable of expanding his abdomen 5 to 10 times its resting size when he is singing to court his mate. The loud droning song of the bagpipe cicada is generally heard in early January, the middle of the Australian summer.

Bladder cicada, *Cystosoma saundersii*: This green cicada has an enlarged, air-filled, resonant abdomen that aids in the production of its song. Evidence indicates that the sound produced by the tymbals is amplified by the resonant abdomen, which functions like an echo chamber. Research conducted on this species in the 1950s indicates that there are three distinct songs: a calling song or free song whose purpose is unknown, a protest song that is made when the cicada is disturbed or threatened, and a courtship song that is used to attract a mate.

Floury baker, *Aleeta curvicosta*: The white markings on this brown cicada have been likened to the dusting of flour evident on a busy chef.

Golden emperor, *Anapsaltoda pulchra*: This is one of Australia's largest and prettiest endemic species of cicada, earning it the regal title of a ruler. Its range is limited to the dense rain forests in a small region of the wet tropics that includes Wooroonooran National Park.

Sandgrinder, *Arenopsaltria fullo*: Native to the coast of Western Australia wherever there is sand, this species is sometimes called the white-banded cicada. It can be found at the Bassendean Sands, Quindalup Dunes, and Spearwood Dunes to name just a few locations. The Latin name can be translated to read "white chantress from the sands," though the female sandgrinder merely listens and does not chant.

Green whizzer, *Macrotristria intersecta*: It is green, and it makes a whizzing sound. Need I say more?

Black prince, *Psaltoda plaga*: Though many individuals of this species sport an overall rich black tone, some specimens have brown or green markings. The female is generally lighter and smaller, which lends greater credence to the masculine common name. The blackest individuals surely are regal insects. The specimens found near Sydney are among the blackest, and the occurrence near that large city makes the black prince one of the most well-known species in Australia.

Black Friday, *Psaltoda pictibasis*: The black coloration of the black Friday is understandable because it is in the same genus as the black prince. Perhaps someone thought it was necessary to name another cicada after a day of the week so the yellow Monday would not be an anomaly.

Brown bunyip, *Tamasa tristigma*: A *bunyip* is a mythical creature from Australian folklore that can be traced to aboriginal mythology. The term is often translated as "a spirit or a devil" and it is believed to inhabit swamps.

Since this harmless and diminutive cicada is found on the fringe of the rain forest as well as in urban areas, its low monotonous buzz is often heard at dusk. Perhaps it was once believed that the song of the brown bunyip cicada was produced by the bunyip of lore. The species emerges in November, earlier than most Australian cicadas.

Razor grinder, *Henicopsaltria eydouxii*: The song of this cicada has been likened to the sound of grinding metal, hence its common name.

Double drummer, *Thopha saccata*: Considered by many to be the loudest insect in the world, double drummers are the largest cicadas in Australia, with a body length of $1\frac{3}{4}$ inches. The sounds are produced by two sets of tymbals, hence the double drums of the common name. The song is described as a loud, piercing, chain-saw-like whine, which fluctuates in pitch.

FISHFLIES: ORDER MEGALOPTERA

Arguably the most spectacular members of the order are the dobsonflies. Identification requests for dobsonflies are among those most frequently asked at What's That Bug? The larva of the dobsonfly is known as a hellgrammite, and despite a tireless search, the origin of the term remains elusive. Nonetheless, even without a source meaning, the name seems appropriate for this large, spiny larva with formidable jaws, capable of drawing blood with its bite. Fishermen are well aware of hellgrammites, and perhaps this colorful and fearsome name was coined by anglers of yore who considered it among the choicest of baits for freshwater fishing. Dobsonflies are among the largest North American flying insects if butterflies and moths are not

considered. Anyone who thought the hellgrammite was a fearsome creature might well be scarred for life after viewing an adult male dobsonfly, whose saberlike jaws can exceed an inch in length. The jaws of the male are not functional for defensive purposes. Though the jaws of the female dobsonfly are notably shorter, they are much more utilitarian, and a female dobsonfly, like the larval hellgrammite, might draw blood should she decide to bite. Adult dobsonflies are reported not to feed; thus they are quite short-lived. They are often attracted to lights, and the large size and fearsome appearance makes seeing one for the first time an unforgettable experience.

ANTLIONS, LACEWINGS, AND RELATIVES: ORDER NEUROPTERA

The net-winged insects are an order of beneficial predators with interesting appearances, habits, and names. Though the adult antlion feeds on nectar from flowers, it gets its name from the predatory habits of its ravenous larva, which can consume large quantities of ants. Antlion larvae live in sandy areas where they dig pits. The antlion, or doodlebug as the larva is sometimes called, buries itself in the sand at the bottom of the cone-shaped pit with only its jaws exposed. When an ant or other hapless insect approaches the edge of the pit, the sand begins to crumble and the insect tumbles into the waiting jaws of the doodlebug. The name *doodlebug* is thought to be a reference to the tracks the larva makes in the sand while searching for a perfect location for its pit. The tracks look as though something had been doodling in the sand. Young children often chant "Doodlebug, doodlebug, come out of your hole," and it is believed that the expiration of breath in proximity to the pit will lure the larva from its

subterranean refuge. Children also fish for doodlebugs with blades of grass, pulling the insects from the sand when they grasp at the blade.

Lacewings, which are occasionally called goldeneyes because of their stunningly metallic eyes, are another member of the family. The larvae of lacewings are voracious feeders that can consume vast quantities of aphids, hence the common names aphidlion and aphid wolf. The owlfly is another neuropteran that gets its name from its protruding compound eyes, which resemble those of an owl.

BEETLES: ORDER COLEOPTERA

The name for this order can be translated from the Greek as "sheath wing," and it refers to the hardened outer wings that are also known as elytra. The membranous hind wings are the actual flying

THE CURIOUS WORLD OF BUGS

wings, and they are protected by the elytra when the beetles are at rest. There are over 350,000 described species worldwide, making up approximately 40 percent of the known insects. The diversity of this order warrants closer scrutiny.

SOME OF MY FAVORITE BEETLE FAMILY AND SUBFAMILY NAMES

Tiger beetles, subfamily Cicindelinae: This ground beetle subfamily includes some of the most gorgeously metallic beetles in the world. These fast-running, fast-flying, elusive predators have earned the name *tiger beetle* because of the skill with which they hunt.

Whirligig beetles, family Gyrinidae: Spinning around and around in circles on the surface of a pond like a whirling dervish, the whirligig beetle can't help but cheer even the most despondent soul.

Burying beetles, family Silphidae: Also known as sexton beetles, after the name for a graveyard caretaker, members of the genus often work in pairs to bury small dead animals like mice or birds. Once the corpse is underground, eggs are laid and the diligent parents care for the larvae by feeding them regurgitated, putrefying flesh.

Rove beetles, family Staphylinidae: The devil's coach horse is an Old World rove beetle that was introduced to North America sometime around 1930. Because of its fondness for eating snails and slugs, it is a friend to most any gardener. Its habit of curling its abdomen over its head like a scorpion is an effective bluff for this harmless species. The frightening appearance, the rearing defensive posture, and the foul odor the insect emits when threatened are apt reasons for its colorful moniker. It isn't difficult to imagine a team of devil's coach horse beetles pulling a demon behind them.

Stag beetles, family Lucanidae: Also known as pinching bugs, stag beetles (genus *Lucanus*) are the aristocrats of the beetle order whose spectacular mandibles resemble the antlers of a stag. These mandibles are

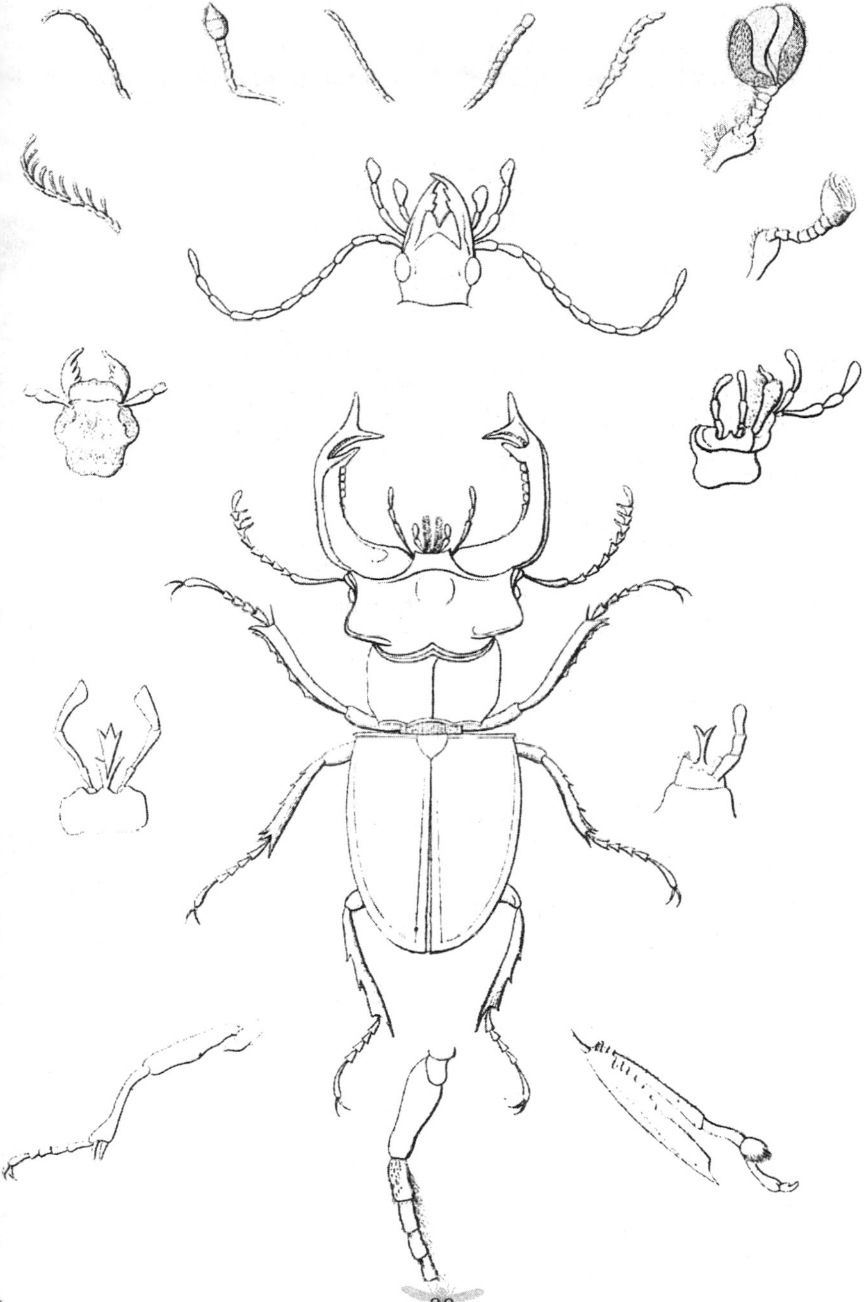

used in sparring contests with other males to obtain dominant status in seeking a mate. Though they aren't dangerous to people, the mandibles may pinch, thus the other common name.

Dung beetles, subfamily Scarabaeinae: Members of this family, also known as tumble-bugs, form a ball out of animal dung, rolling it in a tumbling motion to a suitable location before burying it and laying an egg. This action caused ancient Egyptians to venerate the scarab beetle as a symbol of a god pushing the sun across the sky.

Rhinoceros beetles, subfamily Dynastinae: This subfamily contains some of the world's largest beetles, including the African Goliath beetle, which many consider to be the largest, heaviest modern beetle, though at 4½ inches in length, it is far from the longest beetle in the

world. Males of most rhinoceros beetles are characterized by trophy-worthy horns on their heads. North Americans have to be satisfied with the more modest size of the impressive Hercules beetles (genus *Dynastes*), which grow to a mere 2½ inches in length.

Jewel beetles, family Buprestidae: The gloriously metallic jewel beetles or metallic wood-boring beetles are sometimes used to make jewelry, and they were popular with insect artists in Victorian times. Jewel beetles might be the world's longest lived insects. What's That Bug? has received reports of a golden buprestid emerging from a cutting board that had been in constant use for 8 years, and I have heard of one adult emerging from timber that was milled 51 years earlier.

Click beetles, family Elateridae: Click beetles get their common name from their ability to right themselves if they wind up on their backs. A click beetle is able to snap its body segments against a hard surface, potentially propelling the upside-down beetle several feet in the air to land, it hopes, on its feet. An audible click is made during the action.

Fireflies, family Lampyridae: One of the most nostalgic occurrences on a warm summer night is the appearance of thousands of fireflies or lightning bugs. The former name refers to the light that is generated by the insects as a means of calling to a mate, and the latter common name is a reference to the appearance of the insects just before evening summer thunderstorms. Children often collect lightning bugs in bottles and use them as lanterns to light up the darkness in a tent.

Lady beetles, family Coccinellidae: There is probably no more endearing insect than the lady beetle or ladybug. The iconic red coloration with black spots is reproduced on textiles, household objects, and clothing

around the world, and the beetles are the subject of countless songs, stories, and nursery rhymes. Most species are beneficial predators, feeding on aphids and other insects that feed on cultivated plants. Recently, the multicolored Asian lady beetle has become problematic in parts of the eastern United States because of its aggregating behavior and its instinct to hibernate inside homes. The name *lady beetle* dates to the Middle Ages when the beetle was associated with the Virgin Mary, Our Lady.

Blister beetles, family Meloidae: Also called oil beetles, this family includes the infamous aphrodisiac Spanish fly. Members of the family can exude their hemolymph or blood, which contains the substance cantharidin. Cantharidin can cause blistering on the skin, and there are reports of fatalities if blister beetles are ingested. Despite these frightening statistics, blister beetles, most of which are endemic to the western states, have interesting and complex life cycles.

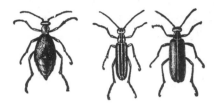

Longhorned beetles, family Cerambycidae: The often strikingly marked and colored beetles in this family are also known as longicorns, capricorns, or sawyers. Many species are characterized by possessing extremely long antennae. In some cases, especially among the males, the antennae are twice the length of the body.

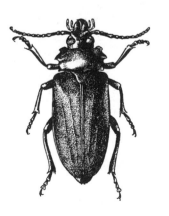

Weevils, family Curculionidae: This is the largest family of beetles, and it includes over 40,000 members worldwide. Many weevils are characterized by having an elongated snout, resulting in the common name snout beetles or bill bugs. There are numerous agricultural pests in this family as well as weevils that feed on stored grains in the pantry.

VELVET ANTS: ORDER HYMENOPTERA, FAMILY MUTILLIDAE

Insects in the order Hymenoptera, which contains ants, bees, and wasps, are quite familiar to most people, and when it comes to names, one of the most colorful groups in the order is that of the velvet ants. Velvet ants are actually flightless female wasps. Most of the members of this family have bold contrasting coloration, especially black and red, and they are covered with hair, giving them the appearance of velvet. The winged males are perfectly harmless, and it is generally wingless females that are seen scurrying quickly over the ground that attract attention. Since she is a wasp, the female velvet ant can pack quite an excruciating wallop of a sting. One large species in the eastern portion of North America is known as a cow killer, because the sting is so painful, it is said that it can kill a cow.

CADDISFLIES (CASEWORMS): ORDER TRICHOPTERA

Caddisflies are relatively insignificant mothlike insects that would not be terribly noteworthy were it not for their unusual aquatic larvae. The larvae of caddisflies are commonly called caseworms— especially by anglers who use them for bait—because of the insect's habit of building cases or mobile homes for themselves. Each species of caseworm constructs its home in a unique shape and from particular materials. Some of these cases are

cylindrical, some are shaped like horns, and some look like the shells of snails. They may be tubular, curved, or rectangular. They might be built from sticks, stones, leaves, grains of sand, or bits of shell joined together by silk that is spun by the larva. One species of caseworm builds a home of sticks set in an ascending square framework, much like the structure of a log cabin with an alternating and overlapping pattern. These homes are both protection and a means of camouflage that helps the tasty larva avoid becoming a meal.

BUTTERFLIES AND MOTHS: ORDER LEPIDOPTERA

Without a doubt, the most recognizable and best-loved insects are the diurnal butterflies, but their primarily nocturnal relatives, the moths, do not generally share this affection. It is believed that the common name *butterfly* originated in England due to the fact that so many of these showy insects are yellow, the color of butter, and that they fly. It is also speculated that both the churning of butter and the appearance of butterflies indicate that spring has sprung.

There is probably more popular literature devoted to butterflies than any other group of insects, so I will introduce but a single species, the red admiral, in an attempt to trace the meaning of its name. The name of this active black butterfly with a single red bar across each wing probably refers to the bars of a naval officer, though the literary master Vladimir Nabokov, a noted and published amateur lepidopterist who often created literary metaphors using butterflies and who also loved wordplay, wrote in *Pale Fire* that the name of this lovely species should be the red admirable. Nabokov also noted in a 1970

interview that in Russia the insect is called the butterfly of doom because large numbers migrated in 1881, the year Tsar Alexander II was assassinated.

Giant Silkworm Moths (and One Sphinx Moth) and Mythology: Family Saturniidae

The silkworm moth family takes its name from the Roman god Saturn, and it can easily be deduced that when insects were being named, this family of very large and very colorful members

was deemed to be the deities among their otherwise generally drably colored and mostly insignificant relatives. Many individuals in this family received names chosen from among the pantheon of Roman and Greek gods as well as from other mythological demigods, heroes, and creatures referenced in ancient texts.

Prometheus moth, *Callosamia promethea*: Named for the god of forethought, the Titan Prometheus who gifted mankind with fire stolen from heaven.

Cecropia moth, *Hyalophora cecropia*: Named for King Cecrops, the first king of Athens who was half human and half snake.

Luna moth, *Actias luna*: Named for Luna, the Roman goddess of the moon.

Polyphemus moth, *Antheraea polyphemus*: Named after Polyphemus, the one-eyed Cyclops blinded by Ulysses in the Odyssey. The reference is obviously to the large eyespots on the wings, though the moth has two spots, whereas the Cyclops had but one.

Io moth, *Automeris io*: Named after the beautiful Io, daughter of the king of Argos. Jupiter was enamored of Io, and jealous Hera turned her rival into a heifer that was guarded by Argus of the hundred eyes. After Argus was killed, Io was pursued around the world by a gadfly.

Atlas moth, *Attacus atlas*: The largest of the silkworm moths, the Atlas moth, a native of Asia, was named after the Titan Atlas, a giant who was condemned to hold the heavens upon his shoulders.

Pandora sphinx, *Eumorpha pandorus*: Giant silkworm moths are not the only insects named after mythological persons. I couldn't resist adding this sphinx moth or hawkmoth, which was named after Pandora, the first woman in Greek mythology who was given gifts from all the gods and goddesses, including a box or jar that was never to be opened. She did not heed the warning and loosed all the plagues and ills upon the world when she opened it. Alas, the Pandora sphinx has been cursed with an undeserved name.

FLIES: ORDER DIPTERA

Lost in the annals of history, probably because it was so insignificant as to not warrant being recorded, someone had the brilliant idea to call the insects in the order Diptera *flies* because they fly. The name of the order refers to the fact that a primary distinguishing characteristic of the flies is that they have two wings rather than four, the number possessed by other winged insects. Though the name *fly* is so ordinary as to seem almost banal, there are many groups of flies that have descriptive names. Crane flies are so named because of their long gangly legs. Bee flies mimic their namesake in both appearance and behavior. Flower flies pollinate blossoms, and fruit flies, which

include numerous agricultural pests like the Mediterranean fruit fly (Med fly, for short), have larvae that feed on ripening fruit. Also grouped in this order are mosquitoes and gnats, and one annoying insect commonly called the no-see-um.

No-see-ums are tiny biting gnats in the family Ceratopogonidae that feed on blood. They are so small that they are able to fit through the fine mesh of window screens. For such a tiny creature, the bite is disproportionately significant. The effects of the painful bite are thankfully short-lived, with inflammation followed by intense itching. Like mosquitoes, a word meaning "little fly" in Spanish, and horse flies, which often bite horses, only the female no-see-um will bite.

Robber Flies in the Family Asilidae

Though they do not abscond with any belongings, robber flies do rob their victims of their lives. The victims include a wide array of other insects. Some groups of robber flies have descriptive names. Hanging thieves are in the genus *Diogmites*, and they often hang by one leg while feeding on prey. Bee killers and bee hunters take their names from their primary prey. One massive bee killer, the Belzebul bee-eater, *Mallophora leschenaulti*, is named for the devil, and the word translates as "lord of the flies."

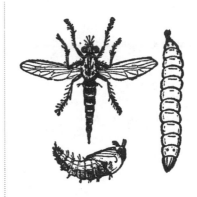

· *Distinguishing a True Fly* ·
from Other Flying Insects by the Name

If we want to follow correct etymological entomology, insects with common names that include a modifying adjective with the word *fly*, like a robber fly, horse fly, house fly, and crane fly are all true flies in the order Diptera. Insects with common names that are compound words that include fly, like butterfly, dragonfly, dobsonfly, or scorpionfly are not true flies, but rather members of other insect orders that just happen to fly. The exception to this rule is the gadfly, a common name for a horse fly that originated in Greek mythology as the creature that tormented the maiden Io after she was transformed into a white heifer by Zeus to disguise his infidelity from his jealous wife, Hera.

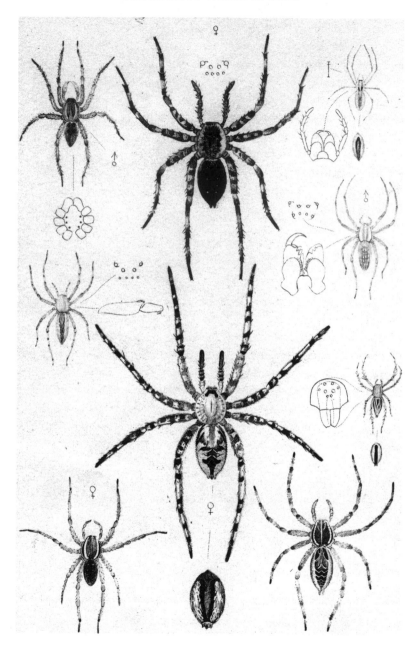

SPIDERS

Spiders are not insects, but they are members of the same phylum, Arthropoda, or arthropods, which are creatures with segmented legs and bodies, and hard exoskeletons. Spiders are further classified as members of the class Arachnida, and they may be identified because they have eight legs and two body parts, a cephalothorax (a fused head and thorax) and an abdomen. All spiders have venom, but only a few species are potentially deadly to humans. Most spiders are reluctant to bite. The word *spider* is derived from the Anglo-Saxon word meaning "to spin," and the class name Arachnida originates from the name of a proud Greek maiden, Arachne, who boasted that her weaving skills were better than those of the goddess Athena. There was a contest, and when Athena couldn't claim the prize, she jealously destroyed Arachne's tapestry, and when the mortal maiden hung herself, Athena took pity and changed her into a spider hanging from a silken thread. Arachne's talent is still evident in some of the symmetrical orb webs woven by certain spiders.

• A Few Spiders with Descriptive Names •

The **black widow spider** received its name because the glossy black female with the identifying red hourglass is documented to occasionally devour her mate.

The **green lynx spider** is a verdant hunting spider that pounces on its prey like a predatory cat.

The **fishing spider** is able to dive beneath the surface of the water and catch minnows and other small fish.

Jumping spiders do not build webs, preferring instead to jump upon flies and other prey.

Orb weavers spin a beautifully engineered, symmetrical web that is the classic web pictured by most people, though many spiders build ramshackle, messy webs.

The **golden silk spider**, a species of orb weaver, is renowned for the strength of the golden silk of its web.

Wolf spiders are hunters that pursue their prey by chasing it down like alpha canines.

Crab spiders resemble crabs and often move in a sideways motion.

Other Arachnids

The class Arachnida includes scorpions, whipscorpions, pseudoscorpions, and solpugids as well as spiders. Poisonous scorpions were important enough for the Greeks to make Scorpio the eighth sign of the zodiac. Nonpoisonous whipscorpions resemble their venomous relatives, and their first pair of walking legs are modified into antennae-like whips. One of the whipscorpions is called a vinegaroon because it produces a weak acetic acid as a defense mechanism, and the acid smells like vinegar. Tiny pseudoscorpions lack venom, but their resemblance to their larger, venomous relatives is indicated by their name. Solpugids have a variety of

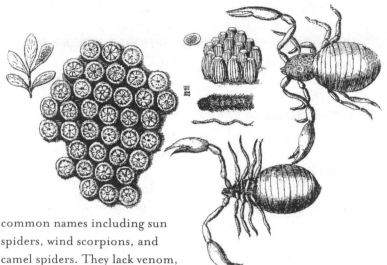

common names including sun spiders, wind scorpions, and camel spiders. They lack venom, but have inspired a slew of myths and falsehoods because of their fierce appearance. It is erroneously believed that large Middle Eastern solpugids (called camel spiders) can leap into the air and disembowel a camel.

CENTIPEDES

The word *centipede* is derived from the Latin for "100 legs," a reference to the great number of appendages. The actual number of legs on different species of centipedes ranges between 20 and 300. These predators have venom, and the bite of several species is considered quite painful. The common house centipede is considered to be harmless.

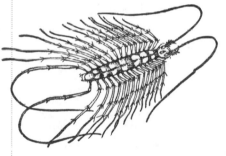

MILLIPEDES

In keeping with the formula for centipedes, *millipede* means "1,000 legs" in Latin. Where centipedes have a single pair of legs on each body segment, millipedes have two pairs on most body segments. Most species have between 36 and 400 legs, and one species is reported to have 750 legs. Though millipedes do not have venom like the predatory centipedes, some species are able to release a cyanide gas as a defense mechanism.

⊙━━✦━━⊙

HORSEHAIR WORMS IN THE PHYLUM NEMATOMORPHA

Horsehair worms are found throughout the world, and they get their common name because they look like a strand of hair from a horse's mane or tail.

Another common name is Gordian worm because of the coiling habit the worms have while mating, making them look like they are tying themselves into knots, a reference to the Gordian knot of Greek mythology, which no one could undo until Alexander the Great cut the knot with his sword. Gordian worms are internal parasites whose typical hosts include crickets, grasshoppers, beetles, and certain spiders.

2

INSECT METAMORPHOSIS
AND SPONTANEOUS GENERATION

EVERYTHING IN THE world changes as it grows and develops. A kitten grows into a cat, and a baby grows into an adult, changing along the way, but infants are recognizably human, and kittens are recognizably feline, and no one would think that an infant might grow into a cat. The unthinkable happens with insects though. Drastic changes happen, in form and habit and in the growing of body parts that were not present in earlier stages. A caterpillar is unrecognizable as an immature butterfly. This transformation is called *metamorphosis*, from the Greek meaning "change form." Metamorphosis also occurs in amphibians like frogs and in aquatic creatures like crustaceans and mollusks, but the acquisition of wings in the adult form, or imago, is unique to insects, making them the poster children for metamorphosis. Not all insects undergo the drastic change that a butterfly needs to transform from a crawling caterpillar into a winged creature of beauty, and there are several degrees of metamorphosis that are recognized by entomologists. Regardless of the degree of transformation of insects (and arachnids and other arthropods), life inevitably begins as an egg.

Insects, generally speaking, are small creatures, and individual eggs are easily overlooked, escaping the notice

of all but the most astute inspector. The female generally lays her eggs where the young will have the best chance of survival, sometimes directly on a food source and occasionally just near a food source; in cases in which the needed food cannot be depended on, the eggs are scattered about in prodigious numbers, ensuring that at least a few of the progeny will successfully reach maturity. The number of eggs produced by an individual varies considerably, though the average insect probably produces between 100 and 200 eggs in a lifetime.

Extremes in the Number of Eggs Produced by Various Insects

Louse fly: The African louse fly loses its wings and spends its adult life sucking the blood from a horse. It produces eggs that develop inside the female's body and that are nourished by her body fluids. On average, each individual produces four or five offspring in her lifetime.

Dung beetle: These scarabs roll a ball of dung across the ground to provide food for each larva. The ball of dung with a single egg is buried. Dung beetles average only 6 offspring each.

In controlled laboratory conditions, they may produce 12 offspring.

Cicada killer: The female cicada killer has the daunting task of paralyzing at least one cicada for each egg she lays, and then transporting that cicada back to her nursery burrow. The average cicada killer burrow contains two to seven individual chambers, each with one egg.

Dobsonfly: A female dobsonfly will lay 2,000 to 3,000 eggs in a single mass.

Australian ghost moth: Currently holding the record among nonsocial insects, a ghost moth from Australia is reported to have laid 29,100 eggs; another 15,000 were discovered when she was dissected.

Queen honeybee: A queen bee may live for several seasons and produce as many as 1.5 million eggs. The University of Florida Book of Insect Records website reports up to 800,000 eggs in 4 years.

Queen ant: According to the University of Florida Book of Insect Records website, "Queens of the African driver ant *Dorylus wilverthi* can lay broods with up to 3–4 million eggs every 25 days."

Queen termite: The greatest insect fecundity prize might go to a queen termite, though different sources supply different statistics. According to the *Encyclopedia Britannica*: "The queen may possibly attain a length of four inches and may lay 4,000 or more eggs a day and many millions during a lifetime of perhaps ten years." That's approximately 14.6 million eggs in a lifetime. A study of termite pillars indicates that the queen of a species of African termite, *Bellicositermes natalensis*, may lay as many as 36,000 eggs a day and is reported to live as long as 50 years. One study indicates she may produce 13 million eggs a year with a lifetime total egg production that may run over 1 billion, though my own math indicates about 650 million, still an impressive number.

AMETABOLOUS DEVELOPMENT: DEVELOPMENT WITHOUT METAMORPHOSIS

The most primitive insects that lack wings, like silverfish, springtails, bird lice, and body lice, do not really change in form as they grow. The hatchlings look very much like the adults, except smaller. Small changes may occur in the form of the body, legs, and other appendages, but they do not merit metamorphosis status. The term *ametabolous* is based on Greek words meaning "without change."

Whether they change appreciably in form, all insects grow in the same manner. Their exoskeleton does not expand, so the skin must be shed, in a process called molting, before the insect can increase in size. They must burst out of their tight skins once their bodies have produced a new exoskeleton. Immediately after molting and before its new skin has hardened, an insect takes in air to ensure that the new skin will expand to the needed dimension to accommodate its larger size.

Gradual Metamorphosis

Insects that undergo gradual or simple metamorphosis have a series of immature stages known as instars, and the larvae are called nymphs. Nymphs resemble the adults in general form and in habit, but they lack wings. After each molt, the instar is larger, and it may change in coloration and markings. During the final instar before becoming an adult, or imago, the nymph develops obvious wing pads that contain the developing wings.

Insects that undergo gradual metamorphosis include the grasshoppers, crickets, katydids, preying mantises, cockroaches, walkingsticks, termites, earwigs, and the hemipterans (cicadas, treehoppers, and true bugs). In almost all of these cases, the young and the adults share a similar habitat and food source,

often existing in peaceful cohabitation, though that is not always the case with the predatory species that might eat one another. Many insects, including aphids and other plant-feeding species, form large colonies. Certain true bugs, like boxelder bugs and milkweed bugs, form large aggregations that include all stages of the gradual metamorphosis process. Cicadas are a bit of an anomaly in the gradual metamorphosis template since the nymphs are subterranean dwellers that feed on the sap from tree roots, whereas the winged adults live in the treetops or in shrubbery and feed on the juices of the stems and twigs of plants.

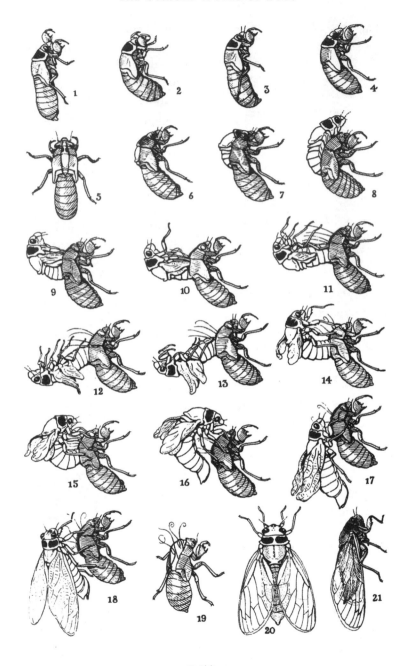

· Vladimir Nabokov ·
and the Coining of the Term Nymphet

Acclaimed author Vladimir Nabokov is credited with introducing the term *nymphet* into the lexicon when he wrote his controversial novel *Lolita* in the 1950s, the story of the middle-aged writer Humbert Humberts's obsession with the pubescent Delores "Lolita" Haze. An amateur entomologist, Nabokov used the term to describe young girls at the point of puberty, just as their bodies are beginning to change and develop the more womanly attributes in the same way that the nymph stage of an insect reveals many of the traits of the adult without being yet matured.

Incomplete Metamorphosis

Insects that undergo a modified gradual metamorphosis, in which the immature stages resemble adults in form but have distinctly different habitats and feeding habits, are said to undergo incomplete metamorphosis. These include many flying insects that have aquatic nymphs known as naiads, such as dragonflies, damselflies, stoneflies, and mayflies. Since the naiads live underwater, they breathe by means of gills, which they lose as adults. The distinction between gradual and incomplete metamorphosis is so subtle that some sources choose to ignore it. Legendary entomologist and author John Henry Comstock was the first to notice and write about the differences.

AN EXCEPTION TO THE RULE: THE MAYFLY

Mayflies are something of an anomaly in the insect world in that they molt twice in the winged

form. Shortly after emerging from the water in preparation for becoming an adult, the naiad, or aquatic nymph, molts and assumes its winged form. This is known as the subimago because within a few hours, it will molt again, shedding even the covering of its wings, at which point it becomes a full adult, or imago.

Complete Metamorphosis

Insects that pass through four distinct phases of development—egg, larva, pupa, and adult or imago—are said to undergo complete metamorphosis. In these insects, the larva bears no resemblance to the adult, and this is probably most apparent in the butterflies and moths. Insects that undergo complete metamorphosis have larvae that molt several times, passing through various instars, much like the nymphs and naiads that undergo less complex metamorphosis. The phase that is unique to complete

metamorphosis is the pupa, a term first used in the 18th century by Carl Linnaeus, the father of modern taxonomy, to describe the dormant state. The word comes from Latin meaning "girl or doll," and Linnaeus was reminded of an infant wrapped in cloth when he coined the term's usage with insects. During this dormant state, the pupa is vulnerable to attack, so many insects produce a protective covering,

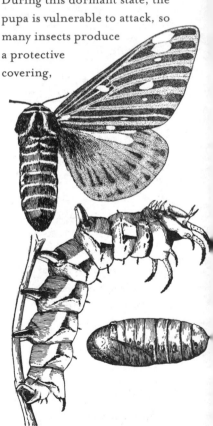

or cocoon, constructed of silk that often incorporates other materials, such as leaves and bits of vegetation, to help camouflage the helpless pupa. Other insects pupate underground in specially constructed chambers, and still others, including most butterflies, pupate in the open. The pupa of a butterfly is called a chrysalis, a word with a Greek root meaning "gold," due to the gold spots and coloration of many butterfly chrysalides. Some insects have limited movement while in the pupa stage. Though not capable of locomotion, many pupae wriggle about, and the abdominal portion of the pupa is especially active. Some of the many insects that undergo complete metamor-phosis are butterflies, moths, beetles, flies, fleas, caddisflies, dobsonflies, lacewings, ants, bees, and wasps.

Hypermetamorphosis

A variation of complete metamorphosis that involves radically different larval forms that look and act differently from one another is known as hypermetamorphosis. Blister beetles exhibit hypermetamor-phosis. Instead of the typical, gradual, larval instar transition found in other insects, the early instars of blister beetle larvae are quite different from later stages in the process. Earlier larval forms are active and predatory, and later forms are more grublike and sedentary.

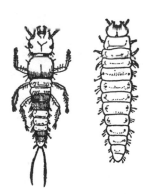

• *Some Common Names for Immature Insects* •

NYMPH: The immature form of insects with gradual metamorphosis, most commonly used with hemipterans like cicadas, treehoppers, aphids, and true bugs.

NAIAD: An aquatic nymph, most commonly referring to dragonflies, damselflies, mayflies, and other flying insects with incomplete metamorphosis.

GRUB: The larvae of many beetles, especially the scarab beetles, longhorned borer beetles, and jewel beetles as well as certain hymemopterans like sawflies and wood wasps are called grubs. These larvae are generally white and curved like a C with short legs. They are often found in rotted wood and in the ground.

WATER TIGER: The predatory, aquatic larva of the predaceous diving beetles are commonly called water tigers.

CATERPILLAR: The larvae of butterflies and moths are known as caterpillars. Many different species, genera, and families have specific names, including the hickory horned devil, the woolly bear, the asp, and the hornworm.

MAGGOT: The larvae of most flies, particularly those that are found in garbage and putrefying matter, are known as maggots. One especially fascinating example is the larva of the drone fly known as a rat-tailed maggot.

HELLGRAMMITE: Dobsonfly larvae, which are prized as bait by anglers, are called hellgrammites.

DOODLEBUG: The immature antlion is called a doodlebug.

APHIDLION OR APHID WOLF: Due to its predatory nature and its diet of aphids, the larva of the lacewing is sometimes called an aphidlion or aphid wolf.

BEELING: An immature bee, though grublike, might be called a beeling.

Spontaneous Generation

Spontaneous generation is a theory developed by Aristotle three millennia ago as a way to explain to ancient Greeks that life developed from inanimate matter on a daily basis. Spontaneous generation explained the appearance of maggots in rotting meat, mice in hay, birds in trees, and lice in human sweat among other seemingly fantastic occurrences. It seemed perfectly logical to the Greeks that as meat rotted, the maggots began to develop spontaneously. The Greeks did not understand that a maggot was actually the immature larva of the fly since a maggot bore no physical resemblance to the fly. There were no scientific laboratories, nor were there sophisticated scientific instruments to assist in the understanding. The only real tool was observation, and the human eye could not detect the flies laying eggs on the putrefying meat. The theory of spontaneous generation was further supported by the speed with which maggots could develop under higher temperatures, and since the Greeks had no means of refrigeration, meat spoiled all the time. Aristotle's theory of spontaneous generation was accepted for nearly two millennia. It took scientists countless experiments and centuries of observation to disprove the theory and to begin to understand the complexities of insect metamorphosis.

It is interesting that the epic Greek poem "The Metamorphosis" by Ovid was completed in the year AD 8, and it describes the creation of the world as well as numerous transformations of the gods into animals and of humans into trees. Alas, the Greeks never made the connection of the classic example of metamorphosis, the caterpillar into the butterfly, despite the fact that the process was immortalized in the title of Ovid's poem.

SCIENTIFIC EXPERIMENTATION DISPROVES SPONTANEOUS GENERATION

Francesco Redi, an Italian physician, published the results of his experiments in 1668. He took six jars and placed an unknown substance in two, dead fish in two, and chunks of raw veal in two. One sample of each was covered with fine gauze, and the other was left uncovered. After several days, maggots developed in the uncovered jars, but not in the gauze-covered jars. He then raised the maggots until flies appeared. He continued the experiments by placing dead flies and maggots in sealed jars with dead fish or veal, and live flies in sealed jars with dead fish or veal, and noticed that maggots developed only in the jars with the live flies.

John Needham, an English biologist, experimented with boiled meat broth in 1745. He sealed batches of broth immediately after boiling, a process that would kill all germs. The sealed broth clouded, causing Needham to speculate that spontaneous generation was responsible, allowing the belief to persist.

Louis Pasteur, the French chemist who gave the world the process of pasteurization, finally disproved spontaneous generation in 1859, when he boiled meat broth in a flask with a curved neck that allowed air to enter, but not particles. The broth did not cloud for an extended period, but once inverted so the particles trapped in the bend could reach the broth, the broth clouded and spoiled. This experiment supported germ theory, the concept that microbes present in the air and other places needed to be introduced to a previously sterile environment before they could reproduce and cause fermentation.

Maria Sibylla Merian

Born in 1647 in Frankfurt, Germany, to a middle-class family of artists and publishers, Maria Sibylla Merian learned to paint and draw during a time when these skills were not taught to young girls. Women were barred from membership in the all-male painting guilds of 17th-century Europe. The development of the silk trade resulted in the introduction of domestic silkworms to Frankfurt, and Merian's family connections gave the budding artist and naturalist access to these fascinating creatures. Gifted with keen observation skills and a powerfully concentrated attention span, Merian watched and sketched the metamorphosis of the insects for hours at a time until she had grasped an understanding of their transformation. By age 13, almost 10 years before published accounts, Merian had already documented the life cycle of the domestic silkworm.

Married at 18 to an artist, Merian moved to Nuremberg where she continued to study and document insect metamorphosis. Merian began by collecting caterpillars from her own garden and raising them in captivity, drawing each stage of transformation over the course of numerous seasons, until the documentation of the entire metamorphosis process of all the various caterpillars and butterflies and moths she was able to find in Nuremberg was complete. She eventually published this as a two-volume set titled *Caterpillars, Their Wondrous Transformation and Peculiar Nourishment*

from Flowers, or simply *The Caterpillar Book*. Though this volume was published numerous times in Merian's lifetime and after her death, the really important piece of observation she produced is her workbook, containing the original drawings compiled through her years of research.

There was one rather puzzling aspect of insect metamorphosis that Merian didn't fully understand. Logically, she understood that the egg hatched into a tiny caterpillar that molted and grew until it was ready for the pupa or cocoon stage, from which an adult moth or butterfly eventually emerged, but sometimes, too often to be ignored, flies or wasps emerged from the pupa. This is well documented in her sketches, but Merian never truly grasped the concept of parasitism in the insect world.

After leaving her husband and embarking on a series of adventures that took Merian to Amsterdam, where she was exposed to ships bringing all manner of exotica to Europe from the jungles of the New

World, she was possessed with a consuming passion to see the Amazon. At the age of 52, in 1699, she sold many of her worldly goods and booked passage to Surinam for herself and her artist daughter. For two years, they stationed themselves in the city of Paramaribo at the edge of the rain forest, where they lived and observed the tropical insects and their life cycles, gathering information for Merian's greatest work, published in 1705: *The Metamorphosis of the Insects of Suriname*, also known as *The Insects of Suriname*.

After her death, harsh critics attempted to discredit the bulk of Maria Sibylla Merian's studies and observations based on some inconsistencies. One of her most famous illustrations from Surinam depicts a tarantula feeding on a hummingbird. The nest of the hummingbird contains four eggs, a known fallacy. The critics also claimed that a tarantula could not catch and feed on a hummingbird, though later research proved this to be a possible, though not a common occurrence. Thankfully, modernity has been kind to

Merian, and her work is appreciated today as being among the most important of its time, and her talent and artistic prowess have been rightfully acknowledged.

A CATERPILLAR BOX: RAISING CATERPILLARS IN CAPTIVITY

Many children love and are intrigued by caterpillars, and it isn't unusual for a youngster to discover a caterpillar and bring it home as a pet. With a little preparation and creativity, one can easily turn this common occurrence into an educational home or classroom science project.

Some important procedures must be followed if you want to raise caterpillars successfully. Start by creating a habitat. A caterpillar box can be built in advance and engineered to last several seasons, or it can be of a more impromptu construction.

A durable wooden frame can be fitted with a window screen or cheesecloth to allow air circulation, and can be reused through successive generations of curious budding naturalists. A quick and cheap caterpillar box can also be assembled from a cardboard box covered with cheesecloth or a window screen on one side. The screening provides ventilation, but it also allows curious observers to look inside the box, and prevents the caterpillar or butterfly from escaping after metamorphosis.

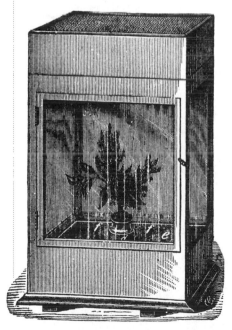

The finer the mesh, the better the protection against parasitoid insects like braconid wasps (see page 74) that could kill the tenant and thwart the anticipated outcome.

Once the habitat is constructed, it is ready for the tenant. Identifying the species of caterpillar is not critical for success, but it will definitely increase the odds. If a caterpillar is discovered feeding on a plant, use that plant to feed the growing larva. Keep the caterpillar supplied with fresh leaves, as it will not feed on dried and dead leaves. If a caterpillar is found wandering far from any greenery, it's possible it has reached the end of its days as a caterpillar, and is getting ready to pupate. Again, identifying the species of caterpillar is very helpful. Species that bury themselves in the ground to pupate need soft, moist soil. It should not be too wet or too dry. If squeezing it causes the soil to clump up without muddying your hands, it is probably perfect for pupation. Some caterpillars will pupate on twigs and others may construct cocoons. There are countless

online resources to assist in the proper identification of caterpillars; try BugGuide (www.bugguide.net) and the U.S. Geological Survey's website, Caterpillars of the Eastern Forests (www.npwrc.usgs.gov/resource/insects/cateast). Lightly mist the caterpillars or pupae to prevent them from drying out, mimicking nature's own precipitation.

Try to duplicate your area's outdoor conditions in the box. At home, the caterpillar box can be kept in a sheltered and unheated garage or shed or outdoors in a shady area. Keep it out of direct sunlight as this may cause the caterpillar to overheat and die, but diffused light is fine. If you can't leave the box outside, the project should still be successful as long as the indoor and outdoor temperatures are not drastically different. In colder climates, once pupation has occurred, it is best to not keep the caterpillar box indoors as this may hasten the emergence of the adult. If a beautiful butterfly or large moth emerges in the middle of winter, it will surely perish before it has a chance to find a mate.

Once the adult butterfly or moth emerges, it can be released into the world after it has been observed. Moths are often more sedate, but butterflies may batter themselves against the sides of the box in an attempt to gain freedom. If one is lucky enough to have raised a female silkworm moth or sphinx moth, the box can be placed outdoors at night to allow nature to takes its course. The female moth will release pheromones, and if any males are in the vicinity, they will be drawn to her scent. The male can be introduced to the habitat and if all goes well, the pair will mate. Once the mated female lays eggs, it will be possible to raise a batch of caterpillars from egg through adult to observe the entire metamorphosis process.

Some Frequently Encountered Butterflies and Moths and Their Life Cycles

In this section you'll find a very abbreviated list of possible tenants for a butterfly box. These caterpillars are frequently encountered, rely on readily available food plants, and are lovely in the adult form. Many caterpillars that are encountered will likely metamorphose into drab moths, which, though equal in the educational benefits, are somewhat lacking in the arenas of drama and spectacle.

The **monarch caterpillar** can be found on milkweed, though it is not the only caterpillar that feeds on that plant. The monarch caterpillar is an attractive insect, marked with thin bands of black, yellow, and white. There are two long feelers on the head end and two shorter feelers on the tail end. This migrating butterfly is found in North and South America and some Pacific islands; it is believed that the population in Australia was introduced.

The **mourning cloak caterpillar** is sometimes called the spiny elm caterpillar. It can be found worldwide throughout the Northern Hemisphere. The caterpillars feed on the leaves of elm, willow, and cottonwood, though several other trees may suffice as food. The spiny caterpillars are black or dark brown with a row of red spots along the back, and they live in a communal web.

Another spiny caterpillar is the **Gulf fritillary**, though in this case the larva is orange with black branching spines and greenish black stripes. There is some variation in the coloration of the caterpillar, but if it is found on passionflower vines, it is assuredly the Gulf fritillary. The caterpillar feeds exclusively on the leaves of that plant, and as cultivation of the vine spreads, so does the range of the butterfly.

The caterpillars of the **black swallowtail** and **anise swallowtail** have a number of similarities. The black swallowtail is found primarily in eastern North America, and the anise swallowtail is found in the western part of the continent. When mature, both caterpillars are green with black stripes and yellow spots, but younger caterpillars of both species are darker with mottled markings. To further confuse the issue, each instar differs in coloration from earlier and later stages. Another unusual physical feature is the presence of the orange osmeterium, a forked scent organ that remains hidden in the folds of skin until the caterpillar feels threatened. Then the osmeterium is revealed, and an odor is emitted that some predators find offensive. Both species feed on the leaves of plants in the carrot family, including dill and parsley, so if a caterpillar is found munching on those plants in the vegetable garden, chances are excellent it is one of these two swallowtails.

If the caterpillar resembles a bird dropping and is found on the leaves of citrus trees, it is likely that it is a **giant swallowtail**. The caterpillar of the giant swallowtail is also called an orange dog. The range of the giant swallowtail includes the regions of North America where citrus thrives and south into Central and South America. Like the previous swallowtails, the orange dog possesses an impressive orange osmeterium.

The **hickory horned devil**, the caterpillar of the royal walnut moth, is the largest North American caterpillar. It has often been compared to a Chinese dragon, and it is a most spectacular creature, nearly 6 inches long with turquoise green coloration, some black markings, four immense black-tipped red horns behind the head, and additional smaller red horns and black horns along the length of the body. The hickory horned devil is most often encountered in September when it descends from the trees, where it has been feeding on leaves; it is found in hickory, walnut, sumac, ash, lilac, persimmon, pecan, and numerous other trees and shrubs. This is one of the moth species that pupates underground, and it is encountered as it searches for a likely location to dig and pupate. Despite its fierce appearance, the hickory horned devil is perfectly harmless.

The **woolly bears** are the caterpillars of various tiger moths, and the banded woolly bear, with its black head and tail ends and rusty orange middle section, is one of the most distinctive. Woolly bears are almost always cute and fuzzy, and they are general feeders that will eat many plants, including grasses, clover, and sunflower leaves. Woolly bears spin a silken cocoon that includes the hairs that are shed before it pupates.

The **luna moth** is considered by many to be North America's loveliest and most distinctive moth, with its pale green coloration, purple veins, and tailed hind wings.

The luna moth caterpillar is lime green with pink spots and a faint lighter stripe along each side. This caterpillar is easily confused with the Polyphemus moth caterpillar, though the adult moths could never be confused. Both luna and Polyphemus caterpillars grow to about 3 inches in length and feed on an extensive variety of leaves from deciduous trees. Both species spin a silken cocoon wrapped in a leaf. The luna moth's cocoon falls to the ground, where it is covered with the insulating leaf litter, which keeps it from freezing in the northern portion of its range. The Polyphemus cocoon sometimes stays attached to the branch and sometimes it falls to the ground. The cocoons of the two species are also somewhat difficult to tell apart.

The highly variable caterpillar of the **Pandora sphinx** may be green, orange, or brown with five large, oval, white or yellow spots along each side. Younger instars have a typical hornworm horn, but this appendage is lost in later instars. The Pandora sphinx caterpillar also has a swollen third thoracic segment into which it may withdraw its head. The caterpillars are most often found feeding on the leaves of grapevines and Virginia creeper.

Enthusiasts who do not have ready access to wild caterpillars can purchase domestic silkworms, *Bombyx mori*. Centuries of domestic cultivation have rendered this moth incapable of surviving in the wild, as it has been bred to produce the highest quality and quantity of silk, which has sacrificed its ability to fly. There are numerous suppliers of domestic silkworms, and the caterpillars can be fed mulberry leaves.

RAISING AQUATIC INSECTS IN CAPTIVITY

An empty unused aquarium or even a small goldfish bowl can be converted into a habitat for raising aquatic naiads, like the larvae of dragonflies and damselflies. It is often possible to find these naiads in ponds, streams, and even in the backyard birdbath or goldfish pond. Water from the source where the naiads are captured is preferable to tap water, but as evaporation occurs, small quantities of tap water can be added to the aquarium. The naiads of dragonflies and damselflies are carnivorous, so feeding them is a bit more involved than feeding caterpillars. Small aquatic insects are readily consumed, but care must be taken that the food does not escape and fly into your home. A mesh or screen cover is ideal for keeping the food in place and preventing the adult from escaping after metamorphosis. Ideally, the water level of the aquarium should be kept about half full, and some sticks can be placed so that they leave the water. When the naiad is ready to metamorphose, it will climb up the stick and transform into a winged adult.

3

FOOD CHAIN

Predators and Their Prey

EVERAL YEARS AGO, a
contributor to What's That
Bug? suggested a column on
predators and their prey, and
that suggestion quickly led to a
popular section on the website.
When it comes to diet, the world
of bugs is made up of extremes.
There are vegans and carnivores,
and even among the carnivores,
there are some very fussy eaters
with very limited diets. While
some insects are indiscriminate
predators that will feed on any
available prey, the number of
species who refuse everything

but one targeted entrée is not a
rarity. This specificity of diet has
resulted in the evolution of
some strikingly unusual
anatomical features to better
accommodate the pursuit of
nourishment.

Generally, insects that
undergo gradual metamorphosis
do not change their diets as they
grow, and an immature preying
mantis will eat the same type of
prey as the adult, though the
adult can handle larger quarry.
Insects that undergo complete
metamorphosis may drastically

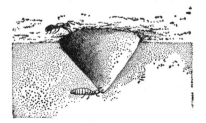

change their diets as they mature. Often the larvae are carnivores, while the adults are vegans. This pattern is especially common among wasps, as you will soon read. This chapter profiles some of the most fascinating host-specific insects that you're likely to encounter and, I hope, provides a glimmer of understanding into the delicate balance of life on our fragile planet.

THE GIANT ICHNEUMON AND THE PIGEON HORNTAIL

Each year in the late spring and early summer, countless identification requests pour into What's That Bug? wondering if the giant ichneumon, a parasitoid wasp in the genus *Megarhyssa*, will either sting a person or damage some prized tree in the garden. The female is usually sighted while she is inserting her lengthy stingerlike ovipositor into the branch or trunk of a tree. The most widely profiled species in guidebooks is

Megarhyssa atrata, a glossy black beauty with a bright yellow head, antennae, and legs. Other commonly sighted species have brown and yellow stripes.

One reason the female giant ichneumon generates so much curiosity is the anatomical feature that terrifies most observers, that huge stinger. Many insects in the order Hymenoptera, which includes bees and wasps, have an ovipositor that doubles as a stinger. Evolution necessitated that the female insect be able to defend herself as well as be able to properly lay her eggs, and the stinging ovipositor resulted. In social insects, like honeybees, the stinger of the sterile worker bees is a modified ovipositor that is no longer used for reproductive purposes. In the case of the giant ichneumon, the stinging feature has been lost, and the ovipositor is used only to lay eggs. This revelation comes as quite a relief since the giant ichneumon's ovipositor can be upward of 5 inches in length, a frightening prospect if you believe you're about to be stung. Sadly, few observers take the time to research the nature of an insect before killing it, and the giant ichneumon is one threatening-looking wasp. When the body and antennae lengths are added, the typical female giant ichneumon can reach nearly 8 inches.

When she discovers a potential food source, she taps her antennae or feelers over the surface of a branch or tree trunk until she senses the quarry below. The target prey for the giant ichneumon is the wood-boring larvae of various wood wasps. Once she senses the larva, she begins drilling with her ovipositor. At the onset of the drilling process, the female raises her abdomen perpendicular to the surface of the wood and the tip of the ovipositor, which is now curled high above the insect, is inserted much as a needle is forced into a cork. Once the wood-boring larva has been reached, an egg is expelled through the ovipositor in, on, or near the quarry. Occasionally a hapless female giant ichneumon

will be unable to extract her ovipositor from the wood, and she dies in the act of procreating.

The host insect of choice for the giant ichneumon's developing larva is a species of wood wasp known as the pigeon horntail, *Tremex columba*, itself a formidable-looking specimen. The adult pigeon horntail is a robust wasp with what initially appears to be a long and thick hornlike stinger, but again, it is the ovipositor of the female. The adult pigeon horntail has a large head with prominent eyes, and the 2-inch-long body is variably colored and marked. It has transparent to smoky brown wings and either a brown or black body, which may be subtly or boldly patterned with yellow stripes and markings. The female horntail lays her eggs in a channel right beneath the surface of the bark. Maple and beech are preferred host trees. Healthy trees are usually ignored, but trees that have been

compromised by fire or flooding or that are weakened or dying because of disease or other insects are selected. As the larvae hatch and grow, they form tunnels and galleries that loop and meander through the heartwood and sapwood of the tree. The giant ichneumon senses the chewing sounds of the pigeon horntail larvae when selecting her drilling site.

Pigeon horntail larvae that are located by the giant ichneumon will provide a source of fresh meat for the developing larva. Once the ichneumon egg hatches, the larva begins feeding on the living tissue of the pigeon horntail larva. Instinctually, it begins eating the musculature and fatty portions of the host larva, leaving the vital organs for the final meal. In this way, a source of fresh meat is always

readily at hand. If the vital organs were consumed first, the host larva would perish and dry out, and the ichneumon larva would starve.

Once the giant ichneumon larva has completely developed, it will pupate in the chamber, and upon emergence as an adult in the spring or early summer, it will chew its way to the surface. Males emerge first and sense the pheromones of developing females; large clusters of males will congregate on the surface awaiting the emergence of the females. Mating has been known to occur before the female giant ichneumon emerges from her pupal chamber. It is believed that neither the male nor the female giant ichneumon feeds as an adult, though there are reports of them taking moisture from droplets that accumulate on leaves.

CICADA KILLER AND DOGDAY HARVESTFLY

Every year in July, What's That Bug? is besieged with requests from the eastern portion of North America to identify a large wasp that builds subterranean nests in sandy soil or clay in people's yards. Other likely locations include golf course sand traps and open fields. The wasp is the cicada killer, *Sphecius speciosus*. Adult females, the larger of the two sexes, are nearly 2 inches in body length. They are very robust wasps. The markings are quite striking, with the head and thorax being a bright rust color while the abdomen is boldly marked with black and broken yellow stripes. The legs are a rusty orange and the wings are a transparent orange. The thick antennae are black and rather long. The stinger of the female is prominent.

Though they are solitary wasps, cicada killers tend to nest in colonies, perhaps because like humans, prime property locations are a definite commodity. When a male cicada killer stakes out his territory, he will aggressively defend it, chasing away other males as well as any manner of insect, bird, quadruped, or biped that happens upon the location. Though he seems aggressive, humans need not worry about the male cicada killer since he has no stinger and is incapable of inducing anything more than fear in the passerby. Once the male cicada killer is successful in having his real estate catch the attention of a house-hunting female, the pair will mate. Having fulfilled his task, the male cicada killer generally dies shortly after mating and the longer-lived female has the sole responsibility of building the nest and provisioning it with food for her brood.

The female builds her nest by using her powerful jaws and legs to excavate a burrow that's 6 or 8 inches deep and roughly ½ inch wide. She pushes the unwanted sand out of the burrow with her rear legs somewhat like a digging dog. Once she reaches the necessary depth, she turns to produce a horizontal tunnel perpendicular to the entry tunnel. This tunnel contains one or more nursery cells. Each cell is used to house a single larva. Once the first cell is constructed, the female cicada killer begins to hunt.

The object of the female cicada killer's search is the annual cicada or dogday harvestfly, either *Tibicen canicularis* or a closely related species. Every year, during the dog days of summer, these 2-inch insects, which resemble large green-and-black flies, can be heard buzzing in the treetops. Their loud buzzing is the song of the male cicada calling to his mate. It is uncertain how the foraging female cicada killer locates her prey, but it is doubtful that it is by the song as her hunting would then be limited to only male cicadas.

Once she locates a cicada, the cicada killer quickly immobilizes

it with her sting. The sting does not deliver a fatal dose of venom, but the cicada is paralyzed in a comatose state, never to awaken. Often this battle results in the cicada killer and her prey falling from the tops of the trees to the ground below, and since the cicada is generally heavier than the wasp, the cicada killer is unable to fly off with her progeny's meal. The cicada killer then drags the immobile cicada back up into the tree so she can glide off in the direction of her nest carrying her heavy load. If she lands in an area where there are no trees or other vertical features that she may use as a launching pad, she will drag the cicada over the ground until she reaches her nest.

When she reaches the nest, she places the cicada into the prepared nursery chamber and lays an egg in it. Sometimes two cicadas are placed in each chamber. The female cicada killer will continue to excavate additional nursery chambers and hunt as long as a steady supply of cicadas can be located. Her nest may contain a single nursery chamber, or several, or if hunting is exceptional, there might be as many as 10 or 20 nursery chambers in her nest.

Much like other wasps that immobilize prey with a sting, the venom of the cicada killer is formulated to keep the cicada alive. Once the larval cicada killer hatches, it begins to feed on the unnecessary body parts, saving the vital organs for the final meal. Once the cicada has been consumed, the larva forms a pupa in the chamber and overwinters in the nest, waiting until the following July to emerge and begin a new cycle and a new generation.

The female cicada killer is reluctant to use her sting on anything other than a cicada, and there are next to no reports of people who have been stung by cicada killers. The reports that do exist are most likely the result of a misidentification since European hornets are similar in appearance and much more likely to sting. Cicada killers have received an undeserved bad rap in what appears to be the result of exterminators capitalizing on homeowners' fear in an attempt to drum up business. Families that are lucky enough to have a nearby colony of cicada killers should observe them and their fascinating life cycles with the knowledge that they are occupying an important ecological niche in the balance of nature.

TARANTULA HAWK AND TARANTULA

The tarantula hawk is the behemoth among North American wasps, with some species reaching more than 2 inches in body length. Most tarantula hawks are blue-black wasps with bright orange wings, and some species have orange antennae. The antennae of the females are curved, and the antennae of the smaller males are generally straight, but it is possible for the female to straighten her antennae, so this is not a definitive method of sexing tarantula hawks. The tarantula hawk, in the genus *Pepsis*, is the largest spider wasp in family Pompilidae. Spider wasps sting and paralyze spiders and either transport them to a nest or leave the paralyzed spider in its own burrow. Since the spider has been paralyzed, it remains alive in a state of suspended animation, and it provides a live food source for the developing wasp larva. Adult spider wasps generally feed on nectar, and the tarantula hawk is particularly fond of the nectar from various species of milkweed.

Sometimes tarantula hawks mate while in the process of gathering nectar from flowers. Male tarantula hawks also engage in a courtship activity known as hill-topping. The male tarantula hawk stakes out territory at the top of a hill and awaits a ready female that will mate. Once he

mates, his job is finished; the female then hunts, provisions the nest, and lays the eggs. The female tarantula hawk flies low over the ground, commonly in desert areas, searching for tarantulas. The tarantula hawk often encounters a male tarantula in search of a mate of his own. When she engages the tarantula in battle, typically the tarantula rears up with its legs, exposing its underbelly to the tarantula hawk's sting. The sting almost instantaneously paralyzes the tarantula. The tarantula hawk then digs a burrow to bury the tarantula after laying a single egg.

It is considerably less work for the tarantula hawk to search out a female tarantula in her burrow. It is believed the tarantula hawk uses her antennae to smell her prey. Once she finds it she lures the tarantula out of its burrow, or she enters the burrow and coaxes the spider out into the open to do battle. The tarantula gets stung on its belly when the spider rears up; sometimes the wasp may try to flip the tarantula by grasping it by the leg or try to approach the wary tarantula from the side so she can deliver her sting. Once the female tarantula is paralyzed, the tarantula hawk drags it back to its own burrow, now a crypt as well as a nursery. The single egg is laid, and the burrow is sealed.

When the egg hatches, the larval wasp has fresh meat to feed on, and like other insects that feed on paralyzed prey, the larva avoids eating the vital organs until there is nothing left. By that point, the tarantula is probably dead. The larva then pupates in the nursery chamber and eventually emerges as an adult after the final metamorphosis.

Since this food chain battle is between two predators, the tarantula hawk occasionally loses the battle and becomes prey for the hungry tarantula instead.

It has been reported that though the female tarantula hawk is not an aggressive species and will rarely sting a human, the sting is nonetheless one of the most painful insect stings of all North American insects. The pain is reported to last only about three minutes, but those three minutes are excruciatingly painful with a burning sensation that leaves no lasting damage.

Tarantula hawks are relatively common in the American deserts of the Southwest, and there are reported to be over 250 species in Central and South America. Some of the tropical species are even larger than our own native species.

AUSTRALIAN SPIDER WASP AND HUNTSMAN SPIDER

Much of what applies to the tarantula hawk applies to a gorgeous Australian spider wasp, *Cryptocheilus bicolor*. This large wasp is black and yellow with chrome yellow wings and legs, a yellow face, and yellow antennae. The primary food for this wasp are the huntsman spiders, large hunting spiders in the family Sparassidae, which are quite common in Australia. Huntsman spiders do not build webs, and they are generally thought of as nocturnal hunters. The spider wasp will overcome all obstacles in an attempt to drag its paralyzed prey back to a prepared burrow, including dragging the spider up and over fences that have gotten in its way.

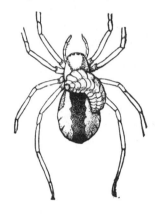

GREAT GOLDEN DIGGER WASP AND KATYDID

Coast to coast across North America, from Canada south into the neotropics, it is possible to encounter the beautiful great golden digger wasp, *Sphex ichneumoneus*. Though not as large as some other predatory wasps, the great golden digger wasp is unique in that it has such a wide range that it is possible for anyone living in North America to encounter it during the summer months.

This highly active wasp is often found in gardens, where it visits flowers in search of nectar. In a vegetable patch, it is apt to frequent the blossoms of onions and related plants, and the umbels of flowering carrots and parsley. In a flower garden, it will visit composite flowers like cosmos, sunflowers, coneflowers, and daisies. Its bold coloration and rapid darting movements are difficult to miss.

This robust wasp is black with a bright orange abdominal first segment. The legs are also a golden orange, there are golden hairs on the head and thorax, and the wings are a smoky amber color. The adult wasp is approximately 1 inch in length.

While the adult great golden digger wasp, like the vast majority of wasps, feeds on nectar, the larvae are carnivores. The helpless larvae are unable to fend for themselves, but the female wasp has developed a refined maternal behavior to best ensure the survival of her progeny. The young feed on katydids, crickets, or cave crickets, depending on the most readily available food in the given location. The female great golden digger wasp hunts the shrubbery or ground for her quarry, and when she espies a meal for her young, she stings it and paralyzes it. She then drags the immobile prey back to her burrow. In cultivated gardens, this burrow is often located between flagstones or on terraced areas. The nursery is a vertical burrow dug down several inches with two to seven chambers radiating outward. The great golden digger wasp places an anesthetized katydid or cricket in each of the chambers and lays a single egg. Much like other wasp larvae, the immature wasp begins by feasting on the expendable body parts and saves the vital organs for last to better ensure that the food will remain fresh and palatable. There is only one generation of great golden digger wasps per year, and the new

generation emerges the following summer. In Florida and other parts of the wasp's southernmost reaches, adults may emerge as early as April, but late July into August are the periods of adult activity in most areas.

Katydids mature at the same time the adult wasps emerge and mate. The mature katydid's large size ensures that the wasp will need to do less hunting, since a single katydid will be able to feed the larva for the entire year.

BRACONID WASPS AND TOBACCO HORNWORM

Many a gardener has found the large green caterpillars of either the Carolina sphinx, *Manduca sexta*, known as the tobacco hornworm, or the five-spotted hawkmoth, *Manduca quinquemaculata*, known as the tomato hornworm, feasting on the leaves of a prized tomato plant. Since the food plants, appearances, and habits of both species are quite similar, these closely related species are often both called tomato hornworms, or tomato bugs. The best means of getting them off of your tomato leaves is to handpick them. Occasionally, a caterpillar will be found that is covered in small white objects that look like silky grains of rice. These are actually the pupae of a tiny wasp in the family Braconidae.

There are more than 1,700 North American species of braconid wasps, and some are quite host specific. Cumulatively, they parasitize such diverse hosts as aphids, bark beetles, and caterpillars. Braconids are important biological control agents for many agricultural pests. Braconids in the genus *Cotesia* are responsible for the parasitization of the tomato hornworm and other caterpillars, including armyworms, cabbage loopers, corn earworms, cutworms, gypsy moth caterpillars, and numerous sphinx moth caterpillars or hornworms.

When a female braconid wasp discovers a hornworm feeding on a tomato plant, she uses her ovipositor to deposit eggs beneath the skin. The eggs soon hatch, and the developing larvae feed on the muscle tissue of the fat caterpillar, avoiding the vital organs. When the wasp larvae have reached their maximum size, they tunnel to the surface and pupate on the outer skin of the caterpillar, sometimes covering the still-living hornworm with viable pupae. Gardeners who encounter hornworms covered with the pupae of braconid wasps are advised not to kill the caterpillars, which are destined to die soon anyway. The best course of action is to allow the pupae to hatch and then a new generation of braconid wasps will help naturally control the population of hornworms feasting on the garden plants by preventing the caterpillars from maturing and producing a new generation.

AMERICAN PELECINID AND MAY BEETLES

There is a very unusual wasp known as the American pelecinid, *Pelecinus polyturator*, and it is the only member of its genus and family north of the Mexican border. This wide-ranging species is also found in Central America and in South America as far down as Argentina. It is unlikely that the American pelecinid could be confused with any other insect. The female can be over 2 inches long, and fully 80 percent of her body length is a six-jointed abdomen. Males are almost never observed. Both sexes have proportionally small wings and the bodies are jet black.

The prey of choice for the female American pelecinid are the larvae of May beetles or June bugs. These beetle larvae are called white grubs and they can be found in soil where they feed on the roots of trees, shrubs, herbs, and grasses. The grubs are C-shaped and white, with a slight bluish cast; they have brown heads and three pairs of brown legs. Gardeners often unearth these white grubs while digging in rich soil near plants. Children are quite familiar with the loud and clumsy flight of the adult May beetles when they are attracted to porch lights in late spring and early summer.

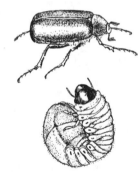

The female American pelecinid uses her long-jointed abdomen as an ovipositor. She plunges her abdomen into the ground where she has located a white grub feeding below the surface. She then lays a single egg on the grub, and when that egg hatches, her larva will feed on the grub. It is believed that the larval wasp kills the white grub quickly and then scavenges its remains.

ENSIGN WASP AND COCKROACH

The ensign wasp, any one of several species of relatively small, insignificant members of a distinctive family, Evaniidae, would probably go unnoticed if it didn't regularly appear in the home. Ensign wasps look vaguely spiderlike, and they have long hind legs like a cricket. Their wings are short and they do not sting. The most distinctive feature is the small, oval abdomen that is attached to the thorax by a petiole, the narrow wasp waist. The abdomen is carried aloft somewhat like a flag, hence the common name. Homeowners often swat at ensign wasps without realizing the benefits of having them in the home. Ensign wasps parasitize the egg capsules of cockroaches, and the larval wasps

feed upon the developing eggs within the capsule, effectively assisting in the control of probably the singular most reviled insect on the planet.

Cockroaches do not lay single eggs, but rather form an ootheca, or egg capsule, that is often carried about by the female cockroach until the eggs hatch. This ensures that the young will have a nearby food source once they emerge. Studies indicate that the female ensign wasp is capable of ovipositing inside the egg capsule of a cockroach while that ootheca is in the care of the female cockroach.

Since ensign wasps are found so often in areas inhabited by humans, it is a fair assumption that they prey on the pestiferous cockroaches, and the presence of an ensign wasp in the home should be welcomed.

CATERPILLAR HUNTER
AND CATERPILLARS

Caterpillar hunters are large, often colorful beetles in the genus *Calosoma*, and both the adult and larval stages feed ravenously upon caterpillars. The fiery searcher, *Calosoma scrutator*, is the species that is most often depicted in guidebooks. The fiery searcher is a magnificent beetle. It is a robust predator, more than an inch in length, and the overall color is a beautiful bright metallic green. Fiery searchers also sport gold, red, and purple iridescences, making then an unforgettable sight. They are found throughout North America, and are among the true beauties in the genus. Other species, such as the fiery hunter and the black caterpillar hunter, are not quite as gaudy but have similar habits and beneficial characteristics.

The forest caterpillar hunter, *Calosoma sycophanta*, was intro-

duced to North America from Europe in 1905 to help control the dreaded European invader, the gypsy moth, because it feeds on its caterpillars. While using these biological methods of control might seem like a good idea, the jury is still out on how many beneficial native caterpillars might fall prey to the forest caterpillar hunter should it not be able to locate its intended meal.

The voracious caterpillar hunters include several widespread species, and some that are more localized. A California species, *Calosoma semilaeve*, is known for irregular population explosions that seem to coincide with years when the caterpillar of the striped morning sphinx, *Hyles lineata*, overrun the abundant spring growth after drenching winter rains. Caterpillar hunters are active predators, and they use their long legs to run about the ground searching for prey. Hunting by the light of day, the adult caterpillar hunter uses its powerful jaws to incapacitate and devour any and all caterpillars it encounters. Occasionally their forages take them inside the home where their large size and aggressive behavior are apt to startle the unsuspecting inhabitants. Caterpillar hunters will not hesitate to chomp down on a human finger, and there has even been one report of a human toe peeking out of a pair of sandals that was mistaken for a juicy larva. The nip that resulted startled the lovely office worker who reported the incident to WhatsThatBug.com, but that nip was perfectly harmless since the caterpillar hunter does not have any venom.

Adult caterpillar hunters have adapted to climbing trees in pursuit of a meal because trees tend to harbor caterpillars. The larva of the caterpillar hunter is also a gregarious feeder and will consume numerous caterpillars in a row without sating its appetite. The larva reaches nearly 2 inches in length, and like the adult, it has powerful jaws. It is interesting that while the adult is a diurnal hunter, the larva tends to be more active at night. Perhaps the nocturnal habits of the larva prevent it from competing for food with the adults.

Caterpillar hunters are relatively long-lived, and there are reports of individuals surviving for up to three years. Adults are sometimes attracted to lights.

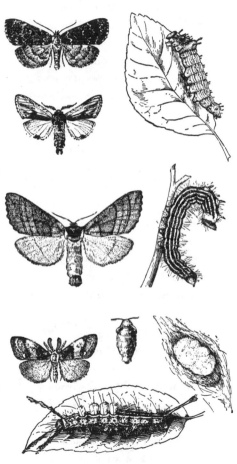

GORDIAN WORM AND POTATO BUG: SUICIDAL TENDENCIES

Anyone with a backyard pool knows full well that large insects and other creatures occasionally fall in and drown, and many of these incidents are purely accidental occurrences, yet there are countless reports of what seems to be suicidal behavior in potato bugs or Jerusalem crickets, a common subterranean insect found in the western portion of North America. The mystery of what triggers a typically burrowing insect to seek out water, be it in a garden pond, swimming pool, or pet's drinking bowl, has one of the most bizarre accounts in the world of predators and their prey.

Back in 2006, What's That Bug? received an amazing historical account from a woman who described her yearly chore of cleaning out the backyard goldfish pond as a child. In 1956, after siphoning out the water to a level of about 4

inches, she stepped in barefoot to discover a strange crunchy layer at the bottom of the pond. What she found was hundreds of dead potato bugs that had mysteriously drowned themselves. There were far too many of them to be explained away by the accidental drowning rationale that one might suggest on discovering one or two insect corpses. The explanation that eventually emerged is definitely fodder for a horror film.

After seasonal rains, observers occasionally discover what initially looks like the long hair from a horse's mane wriggling about in certain bodies of water. They are commonly called horsehair worms because of their physical appearance (up to 2 feet long, but a mere $\frac{1}{16}$ inch in diameter) and the frequency with which they are found in watering troughs used by livestock. Horsehair worms are internal parasites of potato bugs, but other reported hosts include crickets, grasshoppers, beetles, and certain spiders. Though the exact science behind the observation remains a mystery, when the internal parasite has matured, the still ambulatory potato bug is driven to drown itself in water, allowing the horsehair worm to burst out of the body of the host and complete its own life cycle by mating in an aquatic environment.

If the adult horsehair worms are lucky enough to mate, the female may lay an estimated 10 million eggs, though only a small fraction of them will reach maturity. The larvae hatch in the water, but they are not aquatic. They sink to the bottom of the pond or pool, but since potato bugs are not aquatic, the larval worm needs to find another way to reach its eventual host. It is speculated that the larvae are ingested by transport hosts that are not parasitized. The transport host is needed to get the larva somewhere in the vicinity of the potato bug. Once the larva is ingested by a fish, snail, or aquatic insect, the larva forms a cyst, and it will remain in suspended animation until it finds its way to a proper host.

For most of the 10 million offspring, the destination host is never reached, though it is uncertain exactly how long the larva is able to survive in the encysted form. It is possible that it may be able to survive for years.

If the larva is lucky enough to have been ingested by an aquatic insect larva, chances are good that the insect will eventually metamorphose into a winged adult that will fly away from the pond. That winged adult insect will eventually die, and its body will fall to the ground. Since potato bugs are omnivorous insects and readily consume dead insects, there is a million to one chance that the encysted horsehair worm larva will find its way into the digestive tract of a potato bug. Once there, it quickly reanimates and begins feeding inside the body of the host. Once matured, the horsehair worm is thought to release a chemical that causes the irrational behavior in the potato bug, resulting in its pursuit of water, allowing the worm to begin its strange cycle anew.

THE BOT FLY AND ITS MAMMALIAN HOSTS

Also called a warble fly or gadfly, the bot fly in the family Oestridae is an unusual-looking creature that vaguely resembles a bumble bee. The most commonly observed North American bot flies are endoparasites on mammals, such as rodents and livestock. Those in the genus *Cuterebra* are rodent endoparasites and include numerous species that are very host specific, some parasitizing squirrels, others rabbits, others rats, and still others mice. They are fat, clumsy insects that appear to be incapable of flight. These black-and-white bot flies have mottled

markings like a spotted dairy cow, huge heads, and large eyes with red spots.

Life for the adult rodent bot fly begins with the emergence of the winged adult from the underground pupa. Despite a somewhat frightening appearance, adult bot flies cannot bite and do not feed, living only to mate and procreate. Males often emerge first and engage in hill-topping to search for a mate. Males will gather at the top of a hill or on high-growing vegetation and await the emergence of virgin females that are receptive to mating.

Once mated, a female bot fly begins laying her eggs in areas near rodent burrows on stones and vegetation close to the openings, on twigs in the nests, and sometimes along runways traveled by the rodents while foraging for food. A female bot fly may lay as many as 2,000 eggs during her lifetime. The larvae begin to develop within the egg. The body heat of the passing host triggers the hatching of the egg, and the host becomes infested when the larva enters the body through the mouth or nostrils during grooming. Once it has entered the body, the larva travels under the skin to an area on the head, neck, or trunk of the body where it produces a swollen lump. The larva creates a small breathing hole and the gray spiny larva can be viewed beneath the skin through this hole.

The larva grows to about an inch in length and the swollen lump also increases in size. Eventually the matured larva will break through the skin and burrow into the ground to pupate. The presence of one or several bot fly larvae on a host rodent gives the appearance of a sickly animal with multiple tumors, but once the larva leaves the body, the wound quickly heals and the host is not injured by the infestation.

Though they are usually very host specific, there is considerable information available on pets, including cats and dogs, becoming a secondary host for the rabbit bot fly. Pet owners may be horrified at the thought of a cancerous growth on a beloved pet, and when they seek veterinary treatment they find the lump is caused by this insect parasite. The larval bot fly must be excised intact, and the swollen lesion should not be squeezed, as this could cause the larva to break apart, resulting in a secondary infection or possibly an anaphylactic reaction.

There are other genera of bot flies that infest livestock, and sheep and horses are common hosts. Finally, there is a human bot fly that is native to Central America. Though humans are not a primary host, there are a significant number of reports to suggest that the possibility does exist for a traveler to encounter a human bot fly. The female bot fly needs to get her eggs onto the host, generally a cow or dog, and she does this by capturing a blood-feeding insect like a mosquito and then laying her eggs on the body of the mosquito. When the mosquito bites a warm-blooded host, the bot fly eggs hatch upon contact with the body heat, and the larva enters the bite wound or gains access under the skin through a hair follicle. Once under the skin, the larva grows and forms a hard and sometimes painful lesion that may secrete pus. Occasionally, victims report that they can feel the larva moving under the skin, especially while bathing. The Internet has numerous home remedies for the removal of a human bot fly larva, but professional treatment is strongly recommended.

BEE KILLERS, BEE HUNTERS, AND BEES

There is a group of large robber flies in the genus *Mallophora* that are known as bee killers, and others in the genus *Laphria* that are known as bee hunters or beelike robber flies. Both of these genera contain large, fuzzy insects that mimic bumble bees in appearance. These robust flies can grow quite large, and they are aerial hunters capable of capturing on the wing other large insects, including bees and wasps. They strike from above, descending on the unsuspecting

bee while it feeds on a flower. The bee is grasped on the thorax with the powerful hairy legs of the predator that then pierces the body of the quarry and sucks it dry, discarding the empty shell. Bees and wasps have stingers, but when taken from behind in such a manner, they are unable to defend themselves, quickly succumbing to the swift aerial attack.

BLISTER BEETLE AND GRASSHOPPER

Blister beetles are soft-bodied beetles that are most diverse in arid portions of the American Southwest, but representatives of the family are found throughout North America and worldwide. Adult blister beetles are vegetarians that feed on leaves and flowers; they often appear suddenly and in great numbers, feed for several weeks, and then just as suddenly vanish. Though the adults are vegetarians, the larvae are carnivores that have very interesting and complex life cycles.

Adult blister beetles lay their eggs in areas where the larvae are most likely to find a food supply. There are two basic larval food preferences. Some species and genera feed exclusively on the eggs of grasshoppers, whereas others feed on the larva of solitary bees. Once the bee larva has been consumed, the blister beetle larva proceeds to feed on the stockpiled pollen and honey that the bee provisioned for her progeny.

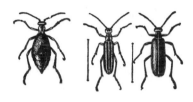

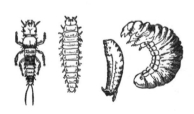

In the case of blister beetle larvae that feed on grasshopper eggs, the female deposits clusters of eggs in holes in the soil. The eggs hatch, and the active larvae search for subterranean grasshopper eggs. Once a clutch of grasshopper eggs is located,

the beetle larva begins to feed on the eggs and soon molts and changes form, becoming a more sedentary grub. The larval stage is short, and within a few weeks, the larva pupates after consuming the eggs. The pupal stage lasts for the remaining portion of the year, until the adult beetles are ready to emerge in great numbers, feed and mate, and continue the cycle again.

There is still considerable research that needs to be done on the life cycle of blister beetles with larvae that prey on grasshopper eggs. There is room for some hypothetical speculation though. Since the adult beetles and the adult grasshoppers, especially in arid regions, would compete with one another for the same food, evolution may have favored blister beetle larvae that help control the grasshopper population, reducing competition among the adults of both species and ensuring the survival of the blister beetles for future generations. This is most significant in light of the swarms of grasshoppers, sometimes called locusts, that can decimate desert flora in a short space of time. After a year with a grasshopper population explosion, a year with a vast number of blister beetles will follow because the active blister beetle larvae have little trouble locating grasshopper eggs.

BLISTER BEETLE AND SOLITARY BEE

A second group of blister beetles, including the antlike oil beetles in the genus *Meloe*, have larvae that prey on the developing larvae of solitary bees. Solitary bees, unlike the social honeybees, have small subterranean nests with few cells for the larvae. Each cell is provisioned with honey and pollen and sealed, and it is in

this cell that the bee larva will grow, develop, and eventually pupate.

Blister beetles that are parasitoids of the solitary bees lay eggs on the stalks of plants with flowers that will be visited by the bees. Other insects including beetles, flies, and butterflies also visit these flowers. The blister beetle larvae hatch and wait on the bloom for a ride, a phenomenon known as *phoresy*. *Phoresy* is the act of one species hitching a ride, often by air, on another insect without doing the transporting insect any harm. Many of the blister beetle larvae will hitch a ride on the wrong host, and if they ride with a fly, beetle, wasp, or butterfly, they will ultimately die.

The lucky blister beetle larvae that rides away from the flower to the nest of the solitary bee will release its hold on the bee once the destination has been reached. The beetle larva then enters the cell that the bee is in the act of provisioning with honey and pollen. Once the cell is stocked with food, the solitary bee lays an egg and seals the cell with the blister beetle larva inside. First the beetle larva eats the bee egg to eliminate its competition, and then it feeds on the food that was provided by the bee. The larva of the blister beetle undergoes hypermeta-morphosis, transforming from a mobile and active larva to a more sedentary larva that grows fat on the nutrient-rich honey. After additional metamorphosis, the adult blister beetle emerges the following season.

LADY BEETLES AND APHIDS

There are nearly 500 species of lady beetles or ladybugs in North America, and all but a few are predatory. The primary prey for most lady beetles are aphids. Since there are at least 80 species of aphids in North America that are considered significant pests of food crops and ornamental plants, lady beetles are among the best insect friends that farmers and home gardeners have. Lady

beetles will also eat other troublesome insects, including mealybugs, scale insects, fly larvae, and caterpillars. They will also eat insect eggs. Though lady beetles are generally thought of as bright red or orange beetles with black spots, they may be spotted or striped, solid, or marked and come in a wide variety of colors, including yellow, pink, black, gray, white, and brown as well as the iconic red or orange. Both adults and larvae of lady beetles are ravenous feeders, and a single individual may consume as many as 50 aphids a day.

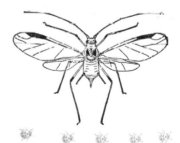

Legend of the Ladybug: A Flight of Fancy

An obscure reference in Frank E. Lutz's *Field Book of Insects*, written in 1918, states: "Why 'Lady-bird' or 'Lady Beetles'? That goes back still further to

---

---

the Middle Ages when these beneficial insects were dedicated to the Virgin and were the 'Beetles of Our Lady.'" That reference resulted in the following flight of fancy and I hope it will provide you with a delightful bedtime story for youngsters.

Mary was a young girl of barely 12 in Bethlehem. She was too young to marry. That year, a caravan of traders arrived from the Orient bearing a heretofore unknown flower, the rose. The rose was uniquely beautiful among known flowers, and the scent of the rose was nonpareil. All the villagers agreed that no flower, no food, nor any fragrance (be it myrrh, frankincense, or patchouli) could match the scent of the rose. That year, there was the potential for an enterprising gambler to make a fortune investing in rose sales. Many men did, including Mary's uncle.

The following year when Mary was barely 13, it was determined by the elder women that Mary was still too young to wed. That year, the rains were good and the crops grew, including the roses. Succulent plant growth was always

compromised by infestation of aphids. That was the year that the aphids discovered the heavenly scent of the roses. The scent drew the aphids to the roses. The winged males arrived first and then the ants carried the fat cows.[*]

The aphids were fruitful, and they multiplied. The gamblers failed to prosper. The aphids became so plentiful that they sucked all the juices from the young rosebuds, causing them to wither. There would be no roses to sell and no profit to be made.

One day, the elder women found that 13-year-old Mary had become a woman and she could marry. They dressed her in white and convinced her uncle not to sell the only rose he had, but to give it to Mary so that she could wear it on her special day.

There was a sea breeze that day. Just as Mary left the house dressed in white and wearing a rare rose to announce to all Bethlehemites that she was a woman and ready to marry, a gust came in off the Sea of Galilee

---

[*] Aphids are often called ant cows because the ants herd the aphids and take them to succulent food sources, and then milk them for sweet honeydew.

and carried shoreward a mass of red beetles with black spots. Smelling the rose, the beetles landed on Mary and covered her skirt in a mantle of red.

Mary calmly continued to walk around the town covered in red beetles, and some people laughed. Just as Mary happened upon her uncle's rose farm, the red beetles sensed the aphids and flew toward the roses, descending on the pests and devouring them.

The red beetles saved the rose-bushes and Mary's uncle's fortune, and it was the day Mary

became a woman. The Bethlehemites exclaimed "It's a miracle!" even those who had laughed. Since that day the red beetles with black spots have been known as ladybugs in honor of Mary.

<hr>

GREEN LACEWINGS AND APHIDS

Green lacewings and their larvae, known as aphid wolves or aphidlions, are another very effective group of predators that

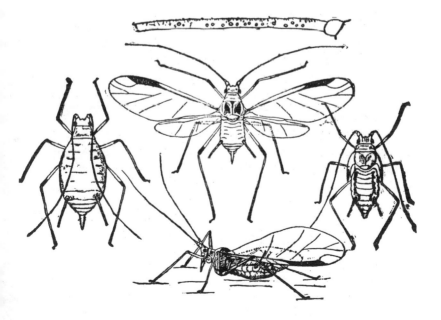

feeds on aphids. Lacewings are considered one of the most economically important predators in the insect world, and they will also feed on scale insects, thrips, whiteflies, and insect eggs.

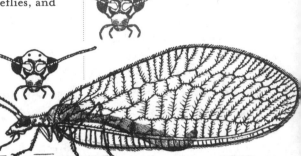

Braconids and Aphids

The braconid wasps (see page 74) may also feed on other insects, though each species of braconid is often quite host specific. There is a group of braconids that feeds exclusively on aphids. The female braconid wasp uses her ovipositor to lay a single egg inside an aphid. Like other internal parasitoid species, the egg hatches, and the parasitic larva feeds on the internal organs of the host. By the time the braconid larva is ready to pupate inside the aphid, the host has usually died and what remains is a bloated form, called an aphid mummy. When the braconid emerges, the aphid mummy is left with a conspicuous hole marking the point of egress.

SUN SPIDERS

Not truly insects, solpugids are arachnids in the order

Solifugae. They are commonly called sun spiders or wind scorpions, though they are neither, and since they contain no venom, they pose no threat to humans, though small creatures had best beware should a hungry solpugid wander near. Larger Middle Eastern species are called camel spiders.

Sun spiders might be the most efficient hunters in the world of arthropods, the phylum that contains insects and their relatives. Sun spiders are most commonly associated with arid ecosystems, and they are nocturnal hunters with a Latin name that translates to "sun fleer." They are fierce predators and voracious carnivores, and sun spiders can run quickly and are able to capture prey with ease. Once they have a small creature in their grasp, they crush and rip the captive to shreds with their powerful jaws. They will feed on any other arthropods they encounter, such as spiders, scorpions, beetles, and caterpillars, and they are also capable of dispatching small vertebrates like lizards.

CAMEL SPIDER: AN IMAGINATIVE MELODRAMA

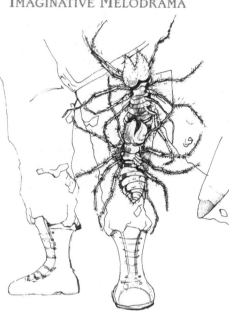

What follows is an embellished description sent to What's That Bug? in November 2003 by Ron, a pilot. Though this letter contains considerable fabrication, I find it highly amusing, and it helps reveal how urban myths come to enter society's consciousness. Stories like this, especially when accompanied by images like the photograph of camel spiders that was widely circulated on the Internet in 2004, have given the camel spider a maligned reputation. That photograph depicts two large Middle Eastern camel spiders dangling in the foreground with the legs of some armed servicemen disproportionately smaller in the background, the result of a wide-angle camera lens and deep focus. Skilled photography produced the illusion of a greatly exaggerated size relationship that was very effective, with frightening results. Here is Ron's colorful account of the biology of a camel spider.

NOVEMBER 3, 2003

Well, here is the nastiest creature God ever placed on this earth. This is what I had to deal with while in Kuwait during Operation Desert Storm. . . . I present to you the infamous "Camel Spider." A vicious insect that lives in the Middle Eastern deserts. Although they are not actually spiders, they resemble a cross between a spider and a scorpion. Also called the sun spider, solpugid, wind scorpion, and a host of other terrible names that do not come close to describing the pure, unadulterated evil that makes up this "hell-spawned" beast. The

Camel Spider can grow to the size of a coffee cup saucer, it can run upwards of 5 miles an hour and jump several feet into the air. That's not the worst part either. The worst part comes when they catch you. (And they will catch you.) Although they are not poisonous, Camel Spiders will inflict a horrible bite. It will jump on you and run up your back until it finds exposed flesh. If you're wearing shorts, it will go for your legs; otherwise it may go all the way up to your face or neck. Its mouth opens four ways to become 4 very sharp fangs. If you are sleeping, it has been known to eat at your face and rip at the flesh. Don't worry, its saliva will numb the wound almost instantaneously . . . by destroying the nerve endings. The saliva also inhibits healing. When your nose grows back, it'll be hideously scarred. I honestly believe if these evil creatures were the size of a German Shepherd, they would rule the earth!

RON

FISHING SPIDER AND MINNOWS

Spiders in the genus *Dolomedes* are commonly called fishing spiders. These are large hunting spiders that do not build webs to trap prey, though they do build webs to provide a safe refuge for their young, a behavior that has earned them another common name: nursery web spider. Fishing spiders are often found near sources of water including swamps, ponds, lakes, and streams. One species in particular, *Dolomedes triton*, commonly called the six-spotted fishing spider, is especially aquatic. The six-spotted fishing spider is generally found near still ponds, and it can run across the surface of the water with ease. The great span of the fishing spider's legs allows the weight to be distributed across the surface area in such a manner that only slight dimples are created on the surface. If threatened, a fishing spider will dive below the surface of the pond and remain submerged for more than 45 minutes,

breathing air that has been trapped by its body hairs. Though it cannot swim, it is able to grasp onto underwater vegetation to keep it from bobbing back to the surface.

Though its primary diet consists of insects caught at the water's edge or snatched from the water's surface where they may have fallen, fishing spiders have been reported capturing small fish and tadpoles with enough frequency to earn them their common name. While it must be stressed that the primary diet of fishing spiders is insects, their ability to walk on water and submerge themselves when necessary has led to the development of angling skills that distinguish them among all other arachnids.

ORB WEAVERS: BUILDING THE WEB

Orb weavers, from the genera *Argiope*, *Araneus*, and *Nephila*, are spiders that build a classic,

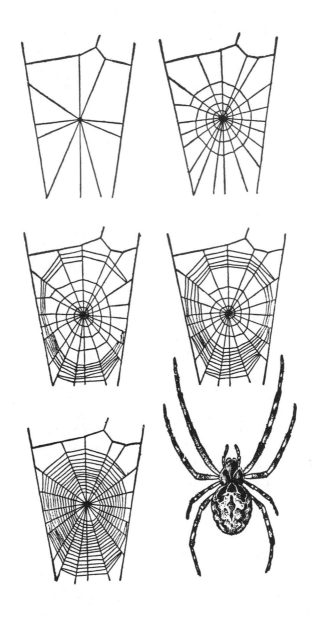

symmetrical web of such wondrous beauty that it is difficult to imagine it to be a deadly snare. It is a triumph of engineering that requires about an hour for the spider to construct, and once completed, the web will entangle any flying creature unlucky enough to fly into it. The web is often spun anew each night in the same or a nearby location. Orb weavers are sedentary spiders that rarely leave their webs because they are clumsy, vulnerable creatures that gracelessly amble along even the most obstacle-free surface.

The spinning of the orb web is best understood when broken down into a series of distinct steps. First the spider defines the location by creating a horizontal bridge line, usually by spinning the silk and allowing the wind to carry it until it catches on a distant object. The bridge line is then pulled taut and the spider strengthens it with additional threads by walking back and forth along the bridge while releasing silk. This bridge line can be reused night after night provided it is not destroyed. The spider then drops a series of anchor lines from the bridge line to form a framework for the web. The spider then lays out the radial lines, beginning with a line dropped perpendicular from the bridge line. All the radii pass through the center point of the web. A nonsticky scaffolding thread is spun that spirals out from the hub of the radiating lines. Finally the orb weaver spins its sticky snare, beginning with the outside and spiraling into the center of the orb, thus completing the web. The web is composed of sticky and nonsticky silk. The bridge and radii are not sticky, but the actual snare that traps the insect is composed of sticky silk.

Once the web is completed, it becomes a very effective trap. Flying insects that become ensnared are quickly wrapped in additional silk and can't break free. They are then injected with venom, and the spider may feed at leisure. The silk of some orb weavers is quite strong, and in August 2007, What's That Bug? posted horrifying images from Texas of a golden orb weaver feeding on a hummingbird it had captured.

Spiders on Drugs

Experiments have been conducted using various drugs, and spiders that have been exposed to marijuana spin a decidedly irregular web, while those given a dose of caffeine create an erratic tangle that bears no resemblance to the elegance of a drug-free orb. Spiders that have been dosed with sleeping pills quit spinning shortly after beginning, and spiders that have been given amphetamines spin webs "with great gusto, but apparently without much planning, leaving large holes" according to *New Scientist* magazine.

Spiders in Space

On July 28, 1973, Anita and Arabella, two cross spiders, *Araneus diadematus*, were launched into space aboard the *Skylab 3* space station, a manned mission. Anita and Arabella were part of a scientific experiment proposed by a Lexington, Massachusetts, high school student named Judy Miles who wanted to know if spiders could spin webs in near weight-

lessness. After an initial adaptation to the lack of gravity during which Arabella spun a sloppy web, both Anita and Arabella produced webs that did not differ significantly from webs spun on earth in terms of the form, structure, and symmetry; however, the consistency of the silken thread spun in space varied in terms of thickness and uniformity. There were no flies for Anita and Arabella to catch in their experimental webs, but the astronauts on board attempted to feed them filet mignon. Both Anita and Arabella died in space, presumably of dehydration, and both of their bodies are preserved at the Smithsonian Institution, memorializing the key roles they played in the understanding of life in outer space.

PREYING MANTIS

The preying mantis is a most formidable predator. Its large size, keen eyesight, and raptorial front legs, which are structurally modified for thrusting and grasping, make it one of the most efficient killing machines in the insect class. In the truest sense of the word, preying mantids do not hunt, preferring instead to sit patiently and wait for prey to fly into range before snatching an insect from the air with lightening speed. Mantids are camouflaged in tones of green and brown to enable them to blend with their surroundings, where they remain motionless in the foliage, forelegs together, as if in an attitude of prayer. Because of this pose the name *praying* mantis is most commonly used with writers, though the secular term *preying* mantis seems more appropriate for this ravenous carnivore.

The preying mantis has a narrow neck that allows its head to rotate nearly completely around. Due to this unique feature, the insect is able to follow the movement of its quarry, as well as to appear to be aggressively staring at a human observer whose movements are also followed with the same rapt attention that is given to a tasty insect morsel. Though poultry is not considered a regular item on this predator's diet, there is at least one image circulating on the Internet of a preying mantis feeding on a hummingbird. Charles L. Hogue, in his book *Insects of the Los Angeles Basin*, cites a report of a preying mantis consuming a mouse, though again, this should not be considered typical fare.

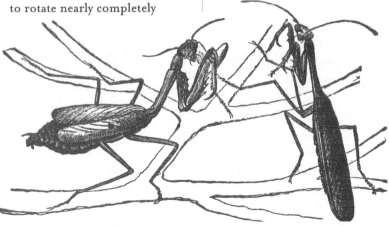

4

BUG LOVE

Mating Rituals and Raising Families

WHEN THE BUG Love page was begun several years ago on What's That Bug? it became an instant hit. All it took was the recategorization of numerous examples of mating bugs and compiling them on a single page, and the readership went rabid in an attempt to have their own examples of the procreative act posted online. The Bug Love page quickly grew to one of the largest sections on the site. Insects locate mates through a wide variety of methods. Some are attracted by scent, others by sight, and others congregate in large numbers near food supplies where sharing dinner can quickly lead to a new family.

MATING AMONG THE EUSOCIAL INSECTS

Termites in the order Isoptera and ants, some bees, and some wasps in the order Hymenoptera are considered eusocial insects in that they live in colonies guided by a swarm intelligence that are descended from one or more fertile queens. Most members of the colony are sterile workers unable to mate and reproduce.

Termites

During mating season when conditions are right, winged virgin female and male termites leave the colony on their nuptial flight. This flight is usually triggered by a sunny day immediately after a spring rain, and neighboring colonies also erupt with winged reproductive adults, which increases the possibility that there will be an exchange of genes, strengthening the genetic characteristics of future generations. These winged reproductive adults are known as alates. Termites, because their powers of flight are so weak, are more often carried by the wind. Once the swarm has left the nest, most of these feeble fliers are eaten by swallows and other insectivorous birds, dragonflies,

and other predatory flying insects, spiders, and a host of other predators.

Upon landing, both the males and females shed their wings and mate, immediately seeking shelter in the soil, woodpiles, dead trees, or possibly the basement or attic of a home. Unlike most eusocial insects, the mated pair of termites continues to rule over the colony as the queen and king, and the king continues to mate with the queen. There may also be more than one royal pair in a colony. The queen termite continues to grow, eventually developing a greatly distended abdomen to better fill her role as an egg-laying machine.

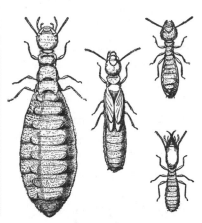

Ants

The mating activity of ants shares many similarities with that of termites. Virgin queen ants are winged adults produced by fertilized eggs, while the winged male ants are produced from unfertilized eggs. Ants select a sunny day for the nuptial flight since rain would put a damper on the event. The mating flight is triggered in neighboring colonies of the same species simultaneously to better ensure cross-breeding and a more diverse gene pool for future generations. The mating act occurs while in flight, far above the surface of the land, and far from the prying eyes of human observers.

Upon consummation, the pair returns to land on the ground and both the male and female forcibly remove their own wings. The male dies shortly afterward, and the female searches for a site for her new nest. The first brood is cared for by the new queen, but

once that brood of workers has reached maturity, the task of feeding and raising the next brood of helpless larvae is turned over to the young workers. Once the colony has reached maturity, the queen will begin to produce a new generation of winged reproductive queens and kings that will fly and start new colonies. There is no plan for succession

in the ant colony, and when the queen dies, the colony perishes with her.

Honeybees

Unlike the other eusocial insects, the queen honeybee is incapable of caring for young or beginning a new hive. A queen bee lives for 3 to 5 years, and her sole purpose is to lay eggs. Fertilized eggs develop into worker bees, and unfertilized

eggs develop into drones, the males whose sole purpose is to mate with a virgin queen. A future queen is not produced from a special egg, but rather, the egg for a future queen is identical to that of a worker. It is the worker bees that determine when it is time to produce a new queen or queens for the hive. They do this when the existing queen ages or dies, or when the colony becomes too large and needs to be divided. The workers start by enlarging the cell in which the egg is laid so that it can accommodate the larger size of a queen. Then they begin feeding the larva of the future queen a diet of royal jelly, a protein-rich substance that is produced by the worker bees. When the time for the emergence of the new queen or queens approaches, the reigning queen departs with some of the workers to start a new colony. As a hive may only have one queen, the first of the new queens to emerge stings any competitors to death, and if more than one queen emerges simultaneously, there is a battle to the death.

Once she has established her ascendancy to the hive, the new queen is ready for her nuptial flight. Summer is the season for the nuptial flight. The virgin queen flies from the hive on a sunny day and seeks a drone congregation area where she will mate with multiple drones, storing the sperm for use for the duration of her life. She may mate with as many as 15 drones, and mating takes place in flight. She may mate with drones from her own hive or drones from nearby hives. The drones perish shortly after mating. Any drones remaining in the hive after the queen has mated are driven out by the workers or killed. The newly fertile queen now takes over as the reigning monarch in the existing hive.

The ordering of Bees:
OR, THE
TRUE HISTORY
OF MANAGING THEM
From time to time, with their hony and vuusе, shewing their nature and Breed.

As also what Trees, Plants, and Hearbs are good for them, and namely what are hurtfull; together with the extraordinary profit arising from them.

Set forth in a Dialogue, resolving all doubts whatsoever.

By the late unparalleled experience of
JOHN LEVETT, Gent.

He who by Bees doth e'er thinke to thrive,
Must order them, and neatly trim his Hive.

LONDON,
Printed by Thomas Harper, for John Harison, 1634.

One can't help but be amused at the certain awkwardness that parents might encounter when using the proverbial bees to explain the facts of life to youngsters. Most female honeybees are sterile workers that do not mate, the male drones are lazy freeloaders whose sole purpose is to fertilize the queen, and the queen loses her virginity to multiple partners in a short period of time in an insect orgy. These are hardly the values that responsible parents would want to teach to their impressionable children.

Wasps

Though they are eusocial insects, the mating of paper wasps, hornets, and yellow jackets does not produce a colony that survives for more than one season. The queen produces reproductive queens and males at the end of the season, and they mate. The males perish, and the mated female hibernates through the winter in a sheltered location. With the onset of spring, the queen begins the construction of a new paper nest and raises the first brood of sterile female workers who go on to expand the nest and care for young. At the end of the season, a hornets' nest may reach the size of a football. When cold weather arrives, the colony including the queen dies and the old nest is never reused. Unlike ants and bees, hornets use the nest strictly for raising young and not for storing food.

COCKROACH COURTSHIP

A female American cockroach signals that she is ready to mate by raising her wings, expanding her genital chambers, and releasing pheromones to attract a mate. This is termed her *calling position*. Males that are attracted to the pheromones flap their wings to indicate interest. Sometimes nibbling, aggressive fighting, and hissing are used in the courtship process. Actual mating begins when the male backs up to the female and deposits sperm. The female retains the sperm and produces an egg case known as an ootheca that resembles a brown capsule. The female carries the ootheca about until she finds an appropriate place to deposit it. She can continue to produce oothecae from a single mating. Sometimes American cockroaches engage in a kind of mating frenzy when there are high population densities. Multiple females assume the calling position, and a flurry of males scurry about with their wings flapping, creating a memorable experience for the observer.

Female Impersonation in Some Tropical Cockroaches

The male insects' goal is to ensure that their DNA is passed on to future generations, and certain insects have devised several unique techniques to accomplish this. Some tropical cockroaches have incorporated sexual mimicry, whereby the manliest of the cockroaches are superseded by female impersonators. At the onset of courtship behavior, a dominant male opens his wings in an attempt to coax a receptive female to mate. If another male observes this activity, he will impersonate the behavior of a female and mount his competitor, fooling the dominant male. Once in this vulnerable position, the dominant male has his wings bitten off by the now aggressive impersonator. After failing to mate, the formerly dominant male retreats to a safe location. He has relinquished the dominant position to a stealth impostor, who may now be able to mate with multiple female partners.

MANTIS MATING ENDS IN CANNIBALISM

The most unique characteristic of preying mantis mating is the possibility that the smaller male becomes a meal as well as a sperm donor. Though there is much information to the contrary, there are enough

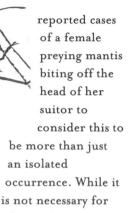

reported cases of a female preying mantis biting off the head of her suitor to consider this to be more than just an isolated occurrence. While it is not necessary for the male preying mantis to be beheaded to have a successful coupling, it does happen. Much like a chicken with its head cut off, the male mantis will continue to perform actions, eventually consummating the act. The male mantis doesn't really make a decision in this matter since he is a slave to his hormones. There is a logical explanation for this extreme behavior. The female requires a considerable amount of nutrition to produce viable eggs. It is a small sacrifice for the male to lose his head, and eventually the rest of his body, to ensure that a healthy future generation gets off to a good start. This is more about the good of the species rather than the survival of the individual.

Northern Grass Mantis: Amazon Society and Virgin Birth

There is a species of preying mantis found in east Texas and in the southeastern states that is most unusual. The northern grass mantis or Brunner's mantis, *Brunneria borealis*, is a species that is represented only by female individuals. Like the Amazons of mythology, there are no known males of the species, and the northern grass mantis reproduces by parthenogenesis or virgin birth. Mating is unnecessary for the species to perpetuate. The closest relatives are found in the extreme southern portions of South America, and the isolation of this species may have somehow contributed to the development of this unusual means of reproduction.

Certain other insects, including many aphids, some katydids, some walkingsticks, some parasitic wasps, and certain bees (remember the drones of honeybees are produced by unfertilized eggs) occasionally or regularly reproduce by parthenogenesis, but in those cases, there are males of the species. Further, their parthenogenic mode of reproduction occurs only at certain times of the year or when males are absent, and future generations are able to reproduce sexually. The northern grass mantis is unique in that there are no males, and reproduction is always parthenogenic.

In sexual reproduction, the gametes (the egg and sperm cells) fuse to form a new being. Genetic material from both the male and the female are passed on to the offspring, creating the possibility of greater genetic diversity in the future generation. For an organism to reproduce sexually, the production of the gametes requires a particular cell division process known as meiosis, which reduces the number of chromosomes in the egg or sperm by half. This is important because when the egg and sperm unite, the resulting cell will then have the correct number of chromosomes for that species. When the other cells in the body divide into two for growth or to replace dead cells, a process known as mitosis,

the two new cells are identical in structure and each has a full set of chromosomes. If the gametes were created through mitosis, then the fertilized egg would have double the number of chromosomes that it should have.

One can only speculate what happened in the case of the northern grass mantis that caused it to become such an anomaly. Perhaps the answer is in the mating process found in other preying mantids in which the female occasionally devours her mate. If the female northern grass mantis was an especially aggressive sexual partner, the males of the species would have become more and more rare. Forced with either species annihilation or adaptation, the northern grass mantis somehow adapted to the shortage of males of the species, so that eventually the male was superfluous to the reproductive process. The eggs of the northern grass mantis do not undergo the additional cell division process, and instead of having half the number of chromosomes, they contain the full number that would be present upon normal fertilization. The sacrifice that is made to the species with this parthenogenic reproduction is that all offspring are female and there is limited genetic variation making the species less able to adapt to changing conditions in the future. It is also possible that there might eventually be a genetic mutation that would again produce a male, and that this Amazon variation may return to sexual reproduction.

DRAGONFLIES AND DAMSELFLIES: THE WHEEL FORMATION

Mature male dragonflies and damselflies are territorial. They establish a location for potential breeding and chase other males away. They then prepare themselves for mating. Males have primary and secondary sexual organs. Sperm is produced

in the primary location at the tip of the abdomen, but it is then transferred in a packet to the secondary location closer to where the abdomen joins the thorax. Once the sperm transfer is completed, the male hunts for a mate, and attraction is primarily visual. Since the eggs will be laid in water and since the body of water attracts the flying insects that the dragonflies feed upon, both sexes are typically present near the nursery location because dragonflies rarely stray far from water.

The male dragonfly captures a female dragonfly by grabbing her around the neck with his anal claspers. These anal claspers are uniquely adapted by each species so that they fit the heads of females of only that species, ensuring that no interspecies mating is attempted. Examination of the male anatomy also helps scientists properly and accurately identify different species of dragonflies. It is believed that certain male dragonflies are able to remove any sperm packets that have been deposited inside the female during a previous mating, ensuring that the last male to mate with a female will be the one whose genes are passed to a new generation.

Once a female is captured in this manner, the pair will fly about in tandem, and it is generally the male that does the flying, allowing the captive female to rest. When they are ready to actually mate, the female dragonfly curls her abdomen around, engaging her sexual organs with the sexual organs of the male, assuming a position described as a wheel formation, or occasionally a heart-shaped formation. This position is unique in the insect world, and it has prompted more than one observer to believe that conjoined twins have been spotted. In some species, the male releases the female after the sperm transfer, though he often continues to guard her as she deposits eggs in the water to ensure that no competing male will attempt insemination.

In the darner dragonflies, the male and female remain in tandem flight position during the egg-laying process. The female submerges to lay eggs while the male maintains his hold on her, flying aloft while she is completely under the surface of the water. It is believed the male's powerful flying prowess is needed to pull the female back to the surface, saving her from drowning.

FLORIDA LOVEBUGS

Because huge swarms of mating March flies are present at certain times in Florida and other Gulf states, these insects have earned the common name of lovebug, or occasionally honeymoon fly. Lovebugs are able to fly about in flagrante delicto, with the pair connected at the abdomen, and it is in this position that they remain for days on end. The smaller male often perishes, and the female continues to fly about with her deceased paramour affixed to her body.

When lovebugs swarm, they can be so numerous on highways that they become a nuisance or even a hazard, if their numbers are sufficient enough to cause obstructed visibility when they splat across the windshield glass. They are even known to cause motor failure if enough bugs are sucked into the radiator air passages, resulting in a reduction of the cooling system. There is much local lore surrounding the lovebug in the Gulf states.

MATING HABITS OF BUTTERFLIES

In a very general sense, the mating habits of butterflies are consistent from species to species. Since they are diurnal, or active during the day, butterflies primarily use their

coloration and markings to attract mates, though occasionally pheromones are involved as well. Once a male and female have matched up, the male couples with the female by engaging the tip of her abdomen with his anal claspers. The pair may stay coupled for several hours, and often fly in tandem. If a female mates with multiple partners, it is the sperm of the final partner that is used first to fertilize the eggs that are laid.

Sexual Organs of Butterflies

When closely related butterfly species that look alike inhabit the same range, the species integrity is preserved by the specialization of the sexual organs. Some species of butterflies are so similar in appearance that dissection of the sexual organs is necessary for people to distinguish one species from another. This differentiation of sex organs also prevents interspecies cross-breeding because the

parts just don't fit together properly. In the 1940s, acclaimed novelist and amateur lepidopterist Vladimir Nabokov published several articles on butterfly taxonomy based on his dissections of a group of butterflies known as the lycaean blues.

Parnassus Butterflies and the Chastity Belt

There is a group of rare alpine butterflies found in mountainous regions of both the New and the Old World called the Parnassus or Apollo butterflies. Many species and subspecies have highly restricted ranges. Sometimes adjacent mountains will host divergent populations of Parnassus butterflies. There are many endangered species in this group, and the desirability among collectors may seriously compromise the survival of some species and subspecies.

Since it is the goal of a male insect to ensure that his sperm fertilizes the female's eggs, and because in most butterflies it is the final mating that successfully does this, Parnassus butterflies have adapted a truly unique method to ensure that the first male that mates with a female will be the victor. After mating, the male deposits a waxy cap, called a sphragis, over the abdomen of the female. This cap acts as a chastity belt, preventing the female from successfully mating again.

SCENT TRUMPS SIGHT FOR MOTHS

Unlike their relatives the diurnal butterflies, most moths are nocturnal (active at night) and cannot use visual cues to identify a prospective mate. As is often the case when one sense is deprived, the creature adapts by having hypersensitivity in another sense, in this case smell. When she is ready to mate, a female moth will release pheromones, strong sexual attractants, that will lure randy males to her side from as far away as several miles. Male giant silk moths have feathered antennae, the better to sense the microscopic airborne pheromones. It is

interesting that the term *pheromone* has recently entered popular culture, and cosmetic manufacturers sometimes add natural aromas to their products to arouse desire in the opposite sex.

The first pheromones to be isolated by scientists were from the domestic silkworm. In 1956, a team of German researchers, after working more than 20 years, identified the female pheromone, which they named bombykol, by removing glands from the abdomens of over 500,000 female moths. Though it has been domesticated for centuries, and it can no longer live in the wild, the domestic silkworm still produces the pheromones used by its wild relatives to attract mates. A newly emerged female giant silk moth like a luna or cecropia may attract numerous males if she is kept outside in a birdcage. Female sphinx moths, or hawkmoths, also have legendary powers for attracting

potential mates from great distances using pheromones.

INSECTS THAT SERENADE THEIR MATES

Many insects audibly call to their mates, including many members of the order Orthoptera. It is the males that call to the females to attract their attention. Insects do not have vocal cords, and they do not use their mouths to produce the sounds. Sound is produced by stridulation or rubbing together of body parts. Many orthopterans have highly specialized structures like rows of toothlike knobs, or fine ridges at the base of the wings or on the legs. Membranous wings vibrate and amplify the sound. Crickets, tree crickets, katydids, and grasshoppers are all orthopterans that produce mating calls. Crickets and katydids rub their two front wings together to produce sound, whereas grasshoppers rub their hind legs

III

together. The other main serenading insects are the cicadas in the order Hemiptera, which produce sound by means of vibrating tymbals, a membrane that is unique to cicadas and a few treehoppers. Cicadas and grasshoppers sing during the day, katydids sing at night, and crickets and tree crickets will sing day or night.

Though it is not considered to be a calling sound, certain flies produce sounds that may be attractive to a mate, and male mosquitoes are attracted to the buzzing of a female's wings. Since those sounds are a result of other activities and they are not used primarily for mating, they are different from the true singing insects. There are most likely other insects that communicate to potential mates through sound, but the vast majority of sounds produced by insects are either so feeble or high pitched that they cannot be heard by humans, although they may be

quite loud to other insects whose hearing organs are different from those of mammals.

LIGHTNING BUGS: A BEACON IN THE NIGHT

Also known as fireflies, lightning bugs are neither flies nor bugs, but beetles with soft bodies. Many species are capable of bioluminescence, or the ability to produce a cold light that serves a variety of purposes. Since larvae are not sexually active, it is possible that the light originated as a warning device to protect the larvae against predators, or it is possible that since the adults use the lights to attract mates, the characteristic first began to appear in the immature larvae as part of the development leading to the adult.

It is well documented that lightning bugs use light to select mates. Because many different species may inhabit the same meadow, it is necessary for a male to be able to distinguish a mate of the proper species.

Depending on the species, the signal is a steady glow, single flashes, or multiple flashes in specific patterns. In many species, the flying male signals and awaits a return signal from a willing flightless female on the ground. The female signals after a specific amount of time has elapsed after the male's signal. Certain cannibalistic species of fireflies have adapted the ability to mimic the courtship flash patterns of other species, waiting on the ground for the eager male to answer the flash and arrive. Instead of a suitable mate, the responding firefly is greeted by a predatory species that devours him.

PARENTING SKILLS OF BUGS

The vast majority of insects do not care for their young after mating and laying eggs. The amount of care given to the young seems to be inversely related to the number of eggs produced by the female. Generally, the more eggs a female produces, the less care she provides for her offspring. Many insects simply scatter eggs about willy-nilly and expect the young to fend for themselves. More caring mothers may place the eggs on or near the source of a larval food plant, and because there is extra work involved in locating the plants, these insects lay fewer eggs. Insects and spiders that capture living food generally lay the fewest eggs, but the individual progeny have better odds for survival.

The eusocial insects that lay countless eggs over the course of a lifetime do not care for their own young. The worker insects in the colony—the sterile bees, ants, wasps, and termites—are the nannies for the young, feeding them and caring for them while the queen needs only to produce more and more eggs. This assessment is a bit unfair to wasps, ants, and termites as the queen usually cares for the first brood, but once she has produced the first generation of workers, she never again turns her attention toward caring for her own children.

The Best Buggy Parents: Burying Beetles

Burying beetles, large black beetles with irregularly shaped red markings, might well get the prize for being the best insect parents, and they are notable in that both the male and female share the entire responsibility of raising a family. Burying beetles or sexton beetles in the genus *Nicrophorus*, including the rare and endangered American burying beetle *Nicrophorus americanus*, locate a small dead animal like a mouse or bird, defend it from other scavengers, and work as a team to bury it completely. A chamber or crypt is created by leaving space between the corpse and the surrounding soil to provide mobility for the parents. Once the carcass is buried, the pair roll it into a ball and remove the hair or feathers. Eggs are laid nearby, and when the eggs

hatch, the larvae are fed prechewed and regurgitated meat from the decaying corpse. Though the parents will share responsibilities, the female does more feeding while the male guards the brood. If one parental unit is removed, the remaining adult will assume all the responsibilities of caring for the young.

Sexual conflicts may occur if a pair of burying beetles locates a corpse that will supply more food than needed for the number of young produced by a single female. There are studies that indicate that burying beetles are monogamous if they have found a small corpse, but if the corpse is larger, the male will emit pheromones in the hope of attracting a second mate. This is advantageous to the male who is able to produce more offspring if he mates twice, but it is not advantageous to the female as there will be fewer nutrients for her brood, hence a lower survival rate. The female will try to discourage the male from attracting a second mate by interfering with his signaling process using a variety of

behavioral tactics that occupy his time. The less time a male spends signaling, the lower the chances that he will attract a second mate.

There is one other interesting feature about burying beetles that contributes to their effectiveness as parents. Any flies that arrived at the corpse before it is buried will have laid eggs, and the maggots will feed on the putrefying flesh of the corpse, reducing the food supply for the growing beetle larvae. Through symbiosis, the burying beetles have evolved a behavior that will reduce the food loss to the maggots.

Many adult burying beetles are found covered in mites. These mites are not parasitizing the beetle though. The mites, which are flightless, use the burying beetle for transportation to a dead animal. This means of transportation is called *phoresy*. The mites feed on the fly eggs and maggots, helping preserve the food supply for the beetle brood. Since the mites use the beetles for transportation, and the beetles benefit by having a preserved food

supply, the relationship is mutually advantageous or symbiotic.

THE FAMILY STRUCTURE OF BESS BEETLES

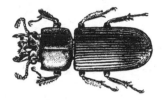

Passalid beetles in the family Passalidae are called by a variety of names, including Bess beetles, Betsy beetles, peg beetles, horn beetles, and patent leather beetles. A pair of Bess beetles begins setting up for a family by locating a nice home. The pair starts by tunneling a series of galleries in rotting wood. The eggs are laid in the excavated galleries. Both the adults and larvae feed on rotting wood as well as adult feces. The young are incapable of surviving on their own, and the wood must be prechewed by the parents. The adults also assist the mature larvae in the preparation of a pupal chamber, which is believed to protect them from cannibalization by their siblings. The first offspring to emerge as adults will assist in the care of the larvae and pupae before mating and setting up their own families. Though it is purely speculation, perhaps the Bess beetles teach good parenting skills to their offspring. This is entirely possible because Bess beetles have a well-developed system of communication. Both adults and larvae are capable of stridulation, or making sounds by rubbing together various body parts. It is reported that they are capable of producing 14 distinct acoustical signals, more than many vertebrates are capable of making. Adults produce sounds by rubbing the upper surface of the abdomen against the wings, and the larvae stridulate by rubbing the third leg against a rough area on the second leg.

DUNG BEETLES MATE FOR LIFE

Certain species of dung beetles form a bond for life to enable them to cooperate together while raising the larvae. Dung beetles, unlike burying beetles and Bess beetles, have a distinct division of labor. The female dung beetle excavates the nursery chamber, and the male guards the home. The male beetle forages for debris, including leaves, flowers, and fruits, that the female adds to the animal feces she collects. The female forms a ball out of the feces and debris and allows it to ripen or ferment for about a week. It is not unusual to see a dung beetle rolling a ball of animal feces across the ground in search of a nesting site. Once the ball of dung has fermented, it is then divided into smaller balls, one for each egg. While the larvae are growing, the male continues to forage for additional dung to provide food for the growing larvae. When pupation time approaches for the larvae, the adults seal themselves inside the nursery to continue to protect the pupae until the adults perish.

PROTECTIVE STINK BUG AND SHIELD BUG PARENTS

There is an Old World family, Tessaratomidae, that is known as the large stink bugs. There are certain species in the family in which the females exhibit an advanced maternal instinct to protect their eggs and young. Some of the members of this family, such as the bronze orange bug from Australia, will guard the eggs and young from any suspected predators, staying with the young until they are nearly grown. Another Australian bug, the cotton harlequin bug in the shield bug family Scutelleridae, also exhibits maternal care of the eggs and nymphs. Some shield bug species in North America

also share this characteristic. These insects are sometimes called parent bugs.

MALE GIANT WATER BUG GUARDS EGGS

Male giant water bugs in the genera *Abedus* and *Belostoma* are anomalies in the insect world in that it is the male that cares for the eggs. The females cement the eggs to the back of the male giant water bug, and he carries them with him until they hatch. These aquatic bugs are highly predatory and have a painful bite. Once the eggs hatch, the giant water bug's paternal duties end, and he spends no time guarding the hatchlings.

SPIDER PARENTING

Many more spiders protect their eggs than do insects. Most web-building spiders will lay one or more egg sacs in their webs and defend them until the spiderlings hatch and disperse.

The green lynx spider is a hunting spider that constructs a web only for her egg sac. The female green lynx will fearlessly defend her unhatched brood from predators much larger than herself, and she will even strike a frightening defensive pose if threatened by humans.

Wolf spiders, which are hunting spiders, go one step further than the web builders. Since they are constantly on the move in search of prey, the female wolf spider drags her egg sac behind her as she runs over the ground. The egg sac is connected by silk from the spinnerets on her abdomen. Once the eggs hatch, the spiderlings climb on board the mother's body and will be transported with her for several days. In this manner, she continues to protect them, and she will also allow them to disperse as they leave her protection one by one, ensuring that they will not compete with one another for food or cannibalize one another.

The highest degree of maternal care exhibited by spiders is probably that of the nursery web spiders, which include the group known as fishing spiders in the genus *Dolomedes*. The nursery web spiders are also hunting spiders in which the female carries the egg sac with her. Unlike the wolf spiders, however, the nursery web spiders grasp the egg sac in their chelicerae, or fangs. Once she has found a suitable location for depositing the egg sac, the female constructs a nursery web, usually among the leaves and branches of a shrub, and she stands guard over her eggs and spiderlings until they disperse, about a week later.

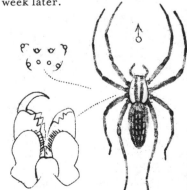

Like most spiders, the brood generally numbers several hundred spiderlings.

WHIPSCORPIONS

After she has mated, a female whipscorpion retreats to a burrow and lays eggs in a silken sac, staying with them until they hatch. Upon hatching, the young climb onto the mother's back and stay with her for about a week. It is believed that the young feed on scraps of food that the mother captures.

Scorpions: Courtship, Mating, Birth, and Care of Young

Scorpions are the most primitive of the arachnids, and they are represented in the fossil record from about 400 million years ago. Scorpions have a complicated courtship and mating ritual, beginning with the pair identifying one another through pheromones. Once they have located each other, courtship begins with the male grasping the female by the pedipalps, or claws, in a sense holding hands with her. The male needs to transfer his sperm, but this is done indirectly as he leads her around until a suitable location for depositing his sperm capsule is located. The pair appears to be dancing together as they move sideways and backward in a *promenade à deux*. It is reported that this courtship may last longer than a day if the male fails to find an appropriate surface for depositing his spermatophore. Once she has mated, the eggs develop inside the female, and she gives birth to her young one at a time. The female carries the young on her back and the young remain with her until at least their first molting.

5

HOUSEHOLD INVADERS

Problematic Bugs in the Home

EVEN THE MOST fastidious homeowner is occasionally startled by a sudden infestation in the kitchen, a glimpse of something unfamiliar scurrying under the bathroom sink, fluttering creatures before the television screen, or some large unidentified flying object on the front porch. While it is true that many of these creatures are benign or even beneficial, there are some species that truly invade the home to damage the structure or its contents, consume our food, attack us and our pets, or annoy us through their shear numbers. These are the true infestations that might require professional exterminators should they escalate beyond a homeowner's control.

I decided nearly a decade ago that What's That Bug?, in its earliest incarnation, needed to demystify these household intruders so homeowners could easily identify the detrimental tenants and eliminate them without harmful chemicals. Simultaneously, I hoped by increasing awareness of the benign or beneficial visitors I could encourage my readers to spare the good guys and either tolerate them indoors or relocate them to the yard. I have broadened my scope significantly since those early days, but my manifesto to aid the homeowner remains true. The following entries strive to identify the most commonly occurring household intruders and distinguish the harmful from the helpful.

Undesirable household intruders, because of their close relationships to domestic environments, seem to have spread across the planet everywhere the creature comforts of civilization have been found. Some species are so closely associated with human habitation that it is impossible to even attempt to identify their ancestral sites of origin.

THREE COCKROACHES

There is probably no more reviled insect on the planet than the cockroach. Of the more than 3,500 known cockroach species, only about 6 are considered pests that infest human dwellings, but those 6 have forever tainted the reputation of the entire order. Their willingness to eat most anything, their preference for sharing human domiciles to the great outdoors, and their alarming reproductive rates are just three factors that contribute

to the universally held perceptions of repulsion for them. Cockroaches are also quite resilient and seem to have evolved to the point that pesticides and other extermination techniques can no longer control them. While there is a general belief that roaches themselves are unclean, they are actually meticulous about their self-grooming. Though I'm not lobbying for the preservation of cockroaches, there is a tendency to overreact when one is noticed in the home by immediately resorting to extermination. It makes far greater sense to identify the cause of the infestation, to clean away exposed food sources, and to specifically target the cockroaches without the spraying of harmful pesticides. It is also worth noting that with certain species, if one cockroach is found, the odds would favor that there are countless more that went unnoticed.

There are three main species of cockroaches that are commonly associated with home and restaurant infestations. They are the German cockroach (*Blattella germanica*), the Oriental cockroach (*Blatta orientalis*), and the American cockroach (*Periplaneta americana*). Of these three, the German cockroach is the smallest and most pestiferous. It is called the German cockroach because it is believed to have been brought to North America from Europe, though it is uncertain if its actual origin is Asia or Africa because it has been associated with human populations since time immemorial. Today it has a cosmopolitan distribution.

The German cockroach averages only ½ to about ¾ inch in length. Since it is one of the smallest cockroaches to infest homes, it can hide in places much too small for the larger species, and it can be more difficult to eradicate. They are most fond of warm, humid locations with a readily available food source, hence their prevalence in kitchens, both private and commercial.

German cockroaches forage for food at night, and they tend to scatter and seek shelter when the lights are snapped on. Meticulous cleaning habits should prevent an infestation of German cockroaches, though apartment dwellers cannot control the sanitary habits of next-door neighbors, and because the German cockroach is such a flat insect, it can easily enter an apartment through the walls via the space near the baseboards. German cockroaches may spread diseases like food poisoning, dysentery, and diarrhea by transporting bacteria from unsanitary locations like garbage cans to formerly clean locations like a sink board. Large populations of German cockroaches are believed to contribute to health conditions including asthma.

The Oriental cockroach grows to about 1¼ inches, and is a dark brown or black species with underdeveloped wings. Its global origin is believed to be either Africa or southern Russia, though it has been associated with civilization for such a long time, it may never be possible to correctly determine a definitive ancestral locale. It is sometimes called a water bug because of its fondness for damp locations in bathrooms and under sinks. Because it will tolerate cooler conditions, Oriental cockroaches are often found in unheated basements, crawl spaces, and sewers. Garbage cans and Dumpsters are prime real estate for the Oriental cockroach. In colder climates, they may seek shelter indoors and become a significant problem. Because of their tolerance to water, they may be able to enter homes through the plumbing. Like the German cockroach, the Oriental cockroach shuns light and prefers to forage nocturnally.

The largest of the common domestic cockroaches is the American cockroach, but despite its name, it is believed to have originated in Africa and to have been brought to the New World on slave ships in the 17th century. The American cockroach is such a large insect it is unlikely to infest a home, but it is frequently found in large numbers in commercial buildings, including grocery stores, bakeries, restaurants, and other places where food is prepared or stored. In the northern United States the species is common in commercial buildings and apartment buildings with steam heating. Indoors, it tends to be most often found in basements, sewers, and drainage systems.

If an individual American cockroach is unwittingly transported to a home, it is far less likely to manifest into an infestation than is the smaller German cockroach.

The American cockroach often amazes observers due to its large size as well as its ability to fly. Though its flight is feeble, it can gain entry into homes by flying in, though it is more likely to enter through the sewer system and plumbing. Enormous numbers of American cockroaches can develop in sewers in favorable conditions, and there are reports of up to 5,000 American cockroaches congregating beneath an individual manhole in an urban setting. According to "Control of American Cockroaches in Sewers," a 1991 study by M. K. Rust, D. A. Reierson, and K. H. Hansgen published in the *Journal of Medical Entomology*, "At least 22 species of pathogenic human bacteria, virus, fungi, and protozoans, as well as five species of helminthic worms, have been isolated from field collected American cockroaches."

• *Five Ways to Introduce a Cockroach to Your Home* •

1. The pizza delivery might contain an extra that was not on the menu.
2. The person next to you at the Laundromat might have transported a hitchhiker that sought shelter in your clean clothes.
3. The grocery store packer might have included something in the bag you didn't buy.
4. That luxurious hotel you stayed in might have had some nonpaying guests that continued to travel in your suitcase.
5. Setting a purse or other bag down in a public restroom may result in a stealth stowaway.

A Cockroach Can Survive for Up to a Month Without Its Head

Many people believe that cockroaches will be the most likely survivors in the event of a nuclear holocaust, and it is common knowledge that when humankind becomes extinct, the cockroach will inherit the earth. The tenacity and resilience of the cockroach is infamous, and this characteristic is further supported in the fact that a cockroach may survive for up to a month without its head. This endurance is due to several physiological reasons. Insects do not breath through their mouths, but through spiracles in the sides of the body, so a headless cockroach can continue to breath. Cockroaches do not have blood pressure the way that warm-blooded creatures do, so decapitation will not result in bleeding to death. Since they are cold-blooded creatures, cockroaches do not require much food, and it is possible for them to survive for a month on a single meal. This characteristic comes in handy since ingestion is performed through the head,

and lacking a mouth, the decapitated insect is unable to take any nourishment. Though deprived of a head that contains the brain, the cockroach, like other insects, has a series of nerve clusters or ganglia in each body segment that allow the headless body to continue to perform simple functions.

CARPET BEETLES

Homeowners around the world are often perplexed when tiny beetles are found congregating near windows in the spring. Often these beetles are carpet beetles in the genus *Anthrenus*. Adult carpet beetles resemble lady beetles in shape, though they are slightly smaller in size. They have variegated patterns on their wings in colors of brown, rust, and white. Adult carpet beetles feed on pollen, and they are congregating near the windows in an attempt to get outside where they can feed.

It is the beetle larvae that should be a cause for concern.

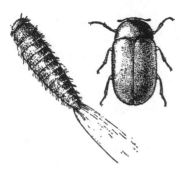

Carpet beetle larvae feed on keratin and chitin, protein compounds that are found in natural fibers like wool, fur, and feathers. Carpet beetle larvae can do considerable damage in the home as well as in museum collections. Before becoming a domestic pest, carpet beetles were found naturally in the nests of birds and mammals where they fed upon shed fur and molted feathers. There is a need for every conscientious homeowner to be able to recognize the larvae of carpet beetles. They are about ¼ inch long with brown and tan bands. The larvae are covered with stiff, erect hairs, and there are two tufts of hair at the rear end of the body. Diligent inspection of items containing natural fibers within the home will prevent damage due to carpet beetle infestation.

BEETLES IN THE PANTRY

There are numerous small beetles that will infest stored food products, most significantly grains and grain products, spices, and even dried mushrooms. All are small and brown in coloration. The average homeowner probably doesn't need to taxonomically identify the species of beetles found in the pantry, because it should be obvious by the location and the numbers encountered that the beetles are feeding on things that we like to eat. There is a reason that preservatives are added to food, and that is to preserve the shelf life. While we would like to think that buying a box of oatmeal will allow us to keep it in the pantry for months (or years), that is not the case. Eventually it will become the source of an insect infestation. The truth is that if we humans will eat it, chances are quite good that other creatures will also find our food to be quite toothsome. There is a reason that every kitchen once contained a flour sifter and every recipe recommended sifting flour three times, because it was necessary to eliminate any unwanted source of protein in the baked goods.

The most common beetles found in the pantry are larder beetles (*Dermestes lardarius*), spider beetles (*Mezium americanum*), granary weevils that often infest rice (*Sitophilus*), drugstore beetles (*Stegobium panaceum*), cigarette beetles (*Lasioderma serricorne*), flour beetles (*Tribolium*), and mealworms (*Tenebrio molitor*).

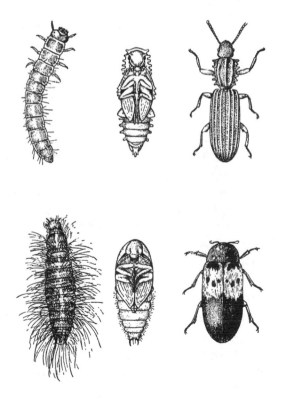

Once an infestation is discovered, the next task is to locate the source. Often overlooked, one of the prime locations is that bargain bag of pet food. Both dried cat food and dried dog food are a likely ground zero for that beetle population explosion. Birdseed should also be checked. The box of cornmeal that gets used once a year for turkey stuffing might be harboring a hidden insect community. Spices are not immune; once I had to throw out some prize Hungarian paprika that was fancied by beetles. Virtually any dried grain product can provide sustenance for pantry beetles, including dry breakfast cereal, rice, oats, wheat, peas, candy, dried fruit, noodles, spaghetti, nuts, and beans. If adult pantry beetles seem to be emanating from your teenager's messy room, try looking under the bed for that stale box of chocolate chip cookies. Finding and eliminating the source of the infestation will generally curtail the problem, but the presence of pantry beetles in one box of cereal may indicate that there is a starter colony in that seemingly pest-free box next to it. It might be safest to discard all potentially infested food and stock up on only what will be eaten in a few months. Keeping food in tightly sealed bottles will help as will refrigerating or even freezing items that are only used sporadically.

Occasionally, the source of the infestation can be a yet unopened box of grain that is sealed in an inner plastic bag. While it's possible that the adult beetle chewed through the plastic and entered through a tiny hole, it's equally possible that the infestation began at the processing plant where large open containers of grain may sit awaiting the packaging process.

Though pantry beetles rarely consume an appreciable quantity of the infested food, their mere presence renders the remaining food unpalatable for the average person. Accidental consumption of the beetles and their larvae wouldn't be so terrible, but there is one frightening possibility. According to author Charles L. Hogue, in his excellent book *Insects of the Los Angeles Basin*,

"Several species act as inter-
mediate hosts and vectors of the
human tapeworms. . . . People
acquire infections by ingesting
beetles containing the larval (or
cysticercoid) stages of the
tapeworm, which will often
remain viable in infested corn
meal and wheat flour that is
undercooked."

MEAL MOTHS OR PANTRY MOTHS

The first clue that you might
have a meal moth infestation
might be tiny moths fluttering
around the kitchen in the dark,
or moths scattering about when
the cupboard doors are opened.
Then, when a container of
oatmeal or a box of stale crackers
is opened by an absentminded
homeowner, the surprise inside
may be a crawling mass of
caterpillars voraciously feeding
on the food within. There are
several species of meal moths
that will infest food, and they
have become so associated with
human habitation, they now
have cosmopolitan

distributions. The most
frequently encountered pantry
moths are the meal moth (*Pyralis
farinalis*), the Mediterranean
flour moth (*Anagasta kuehniella*),
and the Indian meal moth (*Plodia
interpunctella*). All three pantry
moths are in the family
Pyralidae, and they are small
brown and tan species with
distinctive markings on the
wings. Adult moths do not feed
on the grain products, and the
larvae are rather difficult to
distinguish from one another.
You can detect the presence of
moth larvae in grain products by
searching for the telltale signs of
masses of silken webbing inside
food containers and on the
surface of the grain or cases or
tunnels of silk mixed with food
debris. The larvae are about ¼
inch in length and are dirty
white, creamy white, silvery
white, or pinkish white. Stored
cereals, flour, cornmeal,
oatmeal, pet food, birdseed,
herbs, and spices are commonly
infested; meal moths have a
virtually identical diet to that of
the pantry beetles. If one
infested container of food is
found in the pantry, the surest

method of control is to clean out all potentially infested foods and restock, taking care to keep smaller supplies on hand. Food that is stored should be kept in tightly sealed containers and refrigerated if possible.

CLOTHES MOTHS

There are many common misconceptions about moths feeding on clothing that are almost universally believed. There are just a few minute, nondescript moths in the family Tineidae that are actually guilty of doing damage to prized garments. The vast majority of the over 165,000 known moth species worldwide (including the 13,000 North American species) have no interest in eating clothing.

People also believe that the adult moth is perpetrator of the damage, and there are numerous cartoon images of a swarm of moths devouring an entire character's wardrobe while it is being worn, but that is merely material for visual

comedy. The actual guilty culprit is the moth's tiny larva. The larvae do not devour an entire garment, but rather feed in a specific area, often an area that has been stained. Sweat stains are most attractive to the larvae. First the larva is attracted to a stained area on a wool garment, and once it locates a suitable spot, it begins to feed until a small hole is formed.

Another popular misconception is that moths will feed on any and all clothing, but the larvae are very particular about what they will consume. The larvae have no interest in cotton or any synthetic material, feeding instead on fabrics that have an animal origin. Before their association with civilization, the larvae fed on dry animal debris, including fur, skin, feathers, and even horn. Modernity and the advent of wool as a desirable fiber for garments, carpets, and furniture have created an entirely new smorgasbord for these opportunistic feeders.

Many a prized fur and feathered millinery heirloom from Grandma's stylish youth has fallen into moth-eaten dilapidation due to improper storage in the attic. Granddaughter may not mind, and she just might sport that funky sheik cloche in a bold flaunting of convention. More conservative fashionistas probably want to take certain precautions in an effort to preserve their own couture in perpetuity.

MOTHBALLS VERSUS SACHET

A certain sense of nostalgia might be evoked when you catch a whiff of mothballs on an item of clothing, but this once ubiquitous household good has fallen into obsolescence with a certain sector of society. Mothballs contain naphthalene, a substance that has been found to cause health problems in some individuals. Prolonged exposure to naphthalene is toxic, and high concentrations may cause nausea, vomiting, diarrhea, and jaundice. Red blood cells might be destroyed, resulting in temporary hemolytic anemia. These conditions are sometimes present in children who wear clothes that were stored with mothballs but not properly aired or laundered. Fatalities might occur in children who mistake a mothball for candy or in pets that mistake a mothball for a treat. Moth crystals contain paradichlorobenzene, which is even more toxic than naphthalene. It is a suspected carcinogen in animals. Any benefit to using mothballs or moth crystals when storing clothing might be far outweighed by the negative side effects. A sachet, a little pouch of aromatic botanicals, is a safer option.

There are numerous herbs and botanicals that repel moths from the closet. At the forefront is lavender, an aromatic herb with purple flowers that retains its fragrance for years after being dried. Those who spend time in the garden might want to consider growing some of the more commonly used sachet ingredients. After drying the herbs, place them in cheesecloth bags; the scent will appeal to the olfactory sense while keeping garment-destroying species at bay.

My favorite sachet recipe includes equal parts lavender,

rosemary, sage, wormwood (*Artemisia*), and peppermint, all of which thrive in my southern California garden. The herbs are dried, and once sewn into a small fabric pouch, the slightly sharp scent is released each time the sachet is squeezed. One sachet hung on each hanger will protect woolen suits and dresses from marauding moths as well as provide a delightful aroma when the clothing is donned. While the scent of wormwood may be considered medicinal in some circles, it is valued as a key ingredient for repelling insects. Eucalyptus, cloves, cinnamon, bay leaves, and pennyroyal are also effective aromatic insect deterrents that could be included in a sachet. The individual combination may vary with your olfactory preferences.

Cedar is often effective in the protection of valued garments. Cedar chests and cedar closets were popular items that are once again coming back in vogue. If the scent is no longer noticeable, lightly sanding the inner surface of the furniture will often release the aroma. Homeowners not lucky enough to have inherited a

cherished storage unit can buy blocks of cedar to use when storing items that may be attractive to clothes moths.

· Natural Moth · Repellant

1 part dried lavender
1 part dried rosemary
1 part dried sage
1 part dried wormwood
1 part dried peppermint

Combine ingredients. Sew into a fabric pouch and hang with clothing.

TERMITES

Few insects fill a homeowner with fear, or a prospective home buyer with a case of cold feet, faster than the threat of a termite infestation. In certain parts of the country, a home must receive a clean bill of health from an inspector before it can be sold. If termites are found, a visit by the exterminator and the requisite tenting must occur. One might be so bold as to claim that there probably isn't a home in the Los Angeles area more than a few years old that doesn't have some degree of termite damage, though most infestations are so localized that one can live in a home for years and never be aware that the walls contain their own thriving city of insects.

Paranoid insectophobes may fear that in a few short months, if nothing is done about a colony of termites, the entire house may be reduced to a pile of sawdust. It is more likely that decades are required before the damage is so severe as to cause structural weakness. Periodic inspections will help alleviate anxiety about home depreciation due to termite damage.

Termites, also known as white ants, are hidden household intruders that live inside walls and beams, rarely announcing their presence like other more flashy visitors. The first indication that termites might be present is frass,

hexagonal pellets of digested wood that accumulate near the openings of termite galleries. Some termites announce their presence by communicating with one another through audible clicking sounds that may be overheard by a dwelling's human inhabitants. Termites are unable to hear airborne sounds, but the clicking can be sensed as a vibration within the gallery walls. Even if a homeowner fails to notice telltale signs of a termite infestation, once a year, when the conditions are right, termites will announce themselves by swarming. At this time, virgin queens and kings will leave the ancestral home on their nuptial flight, shed their wings, mate, and then select a choice location for setting up their own home and family.

There are two main groups of termites that infest homes and cause damage. Subterranean termites need to maintain contact with the earth and are generally located in wood that forms the foundation of the house. Drywood termites are less of a threat and do proportionally less damage; they are most often found in the dry beams of the attic and other areas that are not in contact with the ground.

ARGENTINE ANTS

In my humble opinion, the single most obnoxious household intruder is the Argentine ant (*Linepithema humile*), also known as the sugar ant or grease ant, since its two preferred foods seem to be sweets and animal proteins. An introduced exotic species, the Argentine ant is the most common ant in southern California. It is believed the Argentine ant was introduced to North America through New Orleans from Brazil in 1891 during the importation of coffee. The ant is a blackish or dark brown species a mere 1/8 inch in length and is conspicuous because of its prodigious numbers and habit of invading homes more than because of its size.

Argentine ants, because of their tiny size, are able to enter homes through minute cracks in the foundation, tiny spaces in windows, gaps in doorways, and other tight spots that invariably exist in every structure. Scout ants constantly patrol for potential sources of food and water, and as soon as a lucky scout returns to the colony with promise of bounty, the hoard begins to invade. The scouts are sneaky, and that single ant usually doesn't attract any attention, but should the home-owner ever let down his or her guard by failing to remove any scraps of food, the invasion will quickly be launched. The tiniest crumbs or sugar grains that escape human notice are a feast for the diminutive Argentine ant. Seemingly endless lines of ants follow the scout's scent trail to the food source or water, marching across baseboards, descending into sinks, filing across the floor, and traveling over walls and tables in their relentless pursuit of nourishment. Their excitement is obvious. The scout's methodical pace is quite different from the eruption of the pillaging army on a mission. That bowl of pet food left on the floor, the sugar bowl, the empty tuna fish can in the garbage bin under the sink, or that lone unwashed greasy pan are quickly covered by a frenzied mass of thousands of marauding invaders.

Interfering with their mission causes them to scatter in every direction. Once off the scent trail, the scattered hoard eventually regroups and continues the assault, though some lone lost individuals may wander aimlessly through the kitchen unnoticed for days.

Those individuals, the new scouts, could discover a previously unknown food source, or possibly discover a new means of entering the home as they wander in search of the base colony. Soon a new scent trail is blazed and the hoard finds ingress via a different location, much to the chagrin of the helpless paying tenant.

The colony itself exists outside of the dwelling, generally in the well-watered gardens and lawns that are tended by residents in the urban and suburban regions of the Argentine ants' adopted range. Shallow nests are constructed in the ground, often under rocks or wood. The galleries of the nest are generally found within 6 or 7 inches of the surface. A unique feature of the Argentine ant colony is that individual nests may contain more than one egg-laying queen. Since the Argentine ants are a warm-weather species, the nests reach a

peak population in late summer, and when the hot, dry season approaches, they begin to invade homes. They also frequently seek shelter indoors at the onset of cooler weather and the beginning of the rainy season when their own nests begin to flood.

Research indicates that spraying aerosol pesticides is not an efficient means of controlling these ants. Individuals may succumb to pesticides, but the colony continues to live on in reduced numbers. The multiple queens then work overtime to produce new workers who will be sent off to locate food. Spraying unnecessary pesticides may result in a temporary fix to the problem, but a systemic solution is necessary to rid the area of the colony. As long as there is a viable queen or queens laying eggs, the marauding hoards will return.

Argentine Ants and Agriculture

Many species of ants develop symbiotic relationships with certain aphids and scale insects. Aphids and scale insects are plant pests that feed on plant juices using their sucking mouthparts. These insects are also known to spread infections between plants. In agricultural areas, aphids and scale insects thrive on crops, and they are the bane of home gardeners as well. The noxious Argentine ant seems to be an especially diligent protector of these plant pest species, defending them from their natural predators and moving them from location to location. In exchange for this protection, the ants are rewarded with honeydew, a sweet, sticky substance expelled through the anus of the aphid or scale insect. Because of this behavior, the Argentine ant poses a significant threat to agriculture in areas where the ant proliferates.

Argentine Ant Supercolonies

Typically, there is a certain degree of competition between neighboring ant colonies with battles developing for dominance of the foraging grounds. This is not the case with Argentine ants. They have spread far and wide from their native South America, and humans have accidentally introduced them to many places on the planet. The species now thrives in the continental United States, Hawaii, Australia, South Africa, New Zealand, Japan, and the Mediterranean region of Europe.

There is considerable research indicating that in three areas of the world—the coastal region of California, the Mediterranean region of Europe, and the western coast of Japan—supercolonies have developed. These supercolonies are unique in that they have a shared genetic background, so that an ant from Los Angeles will be accepted as a member of the colony if it is transplanted to Santa Barbara. The fact that individual colonies with a shared ancestry and genetic uniformity can cohabit has increased the potential threat that the Argentine ant poses as an invasive exotic species that is threatening the biodiversity of the regions where it is flourishing. Since the Argentine ant's introduction to southern

California, native species of ants have declined, and it is believed this is directly responsible for the threatened status of the horned lizards that were once common in the desert areas but are now increasingly more difficult to find. Argentine ants in their native range do not exhibit this genetic uniformity, and they have not developed a similar population density in South America.

Argentine Ant Horror Story 1: Ants Versus Thanksgiving Turkey

Back in the 1980s in my Glassell Park cottage in the hills of Los Angeles's northeast area, when my friend from Ohio, Rosa, was rooming for a spell, we prepared a succulent turkey for Thanksgiving, complete with all the fixings. After the meal, the leftovers went into the refrigerator. The next day, a 1-inch-thick trail of ants could be seen crawling into the kitchen under the space in the front door, and the trail was hurriedly headed toward the refrigerator door, disappearing inside. The door had been left slightly ajar, and it seems that the ants could sense the aroma of the turkey. It was evident by their frantic pace that they had located a tasty feast. When the refrigerator door was opened, we saw, much to our relief, that the ants never made it to the top shelf, where the turkey was placed. They got waylaid by the orange marmalade, which was on the bottom shelf.

Argentine Ant Horror Story 2: Sleeping with the Enemy

Again, back in the 1980s in my Glassell Park cottage, during a year with particularly heavy el niño rains, my living quarters would periodically flood. The yard outside was waterlogged, and the ant colonies were probably flooded as well. Argentine ants are known to relocate if their colonies become submerged, and they settled on some dry real estate inside the cottage. My bed at the time was a twin-size box spring and mattress on the floor. One day, a trail of ants—carrying their eggs, larvae, and pupae—was observed heading toward the bed. On closer inspection, I discovered that the Argentine ant colony had moved into the box spring. Since I did not want to share the bed, I waited for the next sunny day and took the box

---

• Homemade Ant Bait 1 •

1 tablespoon white sugar
1 teaspoon honey
¼ teaspoon active dry yeast
4 tablespoons hot water

Mix all the ingredients together until dissolved. Place in a shallow dish in the path of the ants. The ants will be attracted by the sugar and honey, and the yeast will expand in their bodies, causing them to burst. The bait will be shared with other members of the colony, including the queen, causing the eventual demise of the colony.

> ### · *Homemade Ant Bait 2* ·
>
> 1 tablespoon white sugar
> ¼ teaspoon boric acid
> 3 tablespoons boiling water
>
> Mix all ingredients together. The water must be hot for the boric acid to dissolve. Place the bait in a shallow dish in the path of the ants. The ants will be attracted to the sugar, and the boric acid, once ingested, will cause the ants to desiccate. They will dehydrate and die. The bait will be shared with the other members of the colony, and the effects of the boric acid will be shared, including with the queen. It may take several days, but this should effectively destroy the colony.

spring outside and hit it with a broomstick. The vibrations caused the ants to move out.

THE FLEA

There are over 2,100 species of fleas in the world, and at least 275 species in North America. Fleas are found worldwide, and there is the greatest diversity in temperate climates. Adult fleas feed on the blood of mammals and birds, and they will quickly abandon a dead host as the blood cools. The tiny size and flattened body of the adult flea allow it to move freely within the host's fur, making it difficult to capture and remove it. Fleas can jump 200 times their body length, which allows them to quickly disappear into the surroundings, ready to pounce on the next warm meal that passes by.

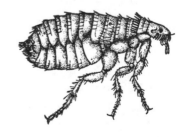

Adult fleas are reported to live for several years, and though they get hungry, they may survive for months without a meal. Fleas typically infest animals that have a regular nesting site, which is why rodents are common hosts and livestock remain relatively free of the pesky critters. The home has many natural potential nesting sites because domestic animals tend to have favorite places to sleep. Most modern households have at least one cat or dog, and if Fluffy and Fido occasionally go outdoors, chances are good they return with a few unwanted passengers.

The average homeowner probably couldn't care less what species of flea has invaded the home, but two of the likeliest candidates are the cat flea, *Ctenocephalides felis*, and the dog flea, *Ctenocephalides canis*. It is interesting that the cat flea will infest dogs and the dog flea will infest cats, and both species will infest homes and bite humans. Flea bites are most irritating, often causing inflammation and itching that may last for weeks.

The secret to ridding the

• *Historic Flea Repellant: The Four Thieves* •

This recipe for antiseptic vinegar is known as the "Four Thieves" because it is said that pillagers in the Dark Ages rubbed their bodies with it to keep away the fleas when robbing plague victims.

Several sprigs of wormwood
Several sprigs of lavender
Several sprigs of rosemary
Several sprigs of sage

Add herbs to a gallon of white vinegar and place in the sun for a few weeks. The concoction will last for years. Add to the bath for a refreshing tonic or sprinkle your pet to ward off fleas. Sprinkle in areas where fleas abound.

home of fleas is to get them where the larvae are living. Larval fleas do not feed on blood, but rather eat organic debris in the host's nest. Frequently changing the pet's bedding, vacuuming the furniture and carpet, and emptying the vacuum cleaner frequently will help minimize the population of fleas. Replacing wall-to-wall carpet with floor rugs that can be taken outside and shaken or beaten will make a great difference if you're not invested in a permanent floor covering.

BED BUGS: MORE THAN A BEDTIME RHYME

Many a parent in days of yore sent the children off to sleep with the familiar rhyme "Sleep tight. Don't let the bed bugs bite." While that blessing seems long outdated, the fact of the matter is that in recent years,

infestations of bed bugs have become commonplace in many urban centers around the world, including New York and Los Angeles.

The bed bug is an oval, flattened, brown insect that grows to about ⅓ inch in length. Bed bugs have a cosmopolitan distribution, and they are found everywhere their human host calls home. They may be found year-round, and both adults and immature bed bugs feed on human blood, stealthily invading the bed while the unsuspecting victim is fast asleep. While some victims find the initial bite to be quite painful, often the first indication that there is a bloodsucker in the room is the presence of dark stains on the sheets, a result of the blood infused excrement of the attacker. An annoying and persistent itching often follows the bites the next day, and heavy infestations

· Tips for Keeping Bed Bugs Out of the Bed ·

Flipping the mattress and box spring daily will aid in the detection of bed bugs that would otherwise have but a short stroll to feed on a sleeping victim. If bed bugs are known to be present, keeping the bedding tight, as in the childhood rhyme, will help prevent bites. Bedding including blankets, sheets, and quilts should be kept off the floor, and a tightly made bed is a significant deterrent to keeping the bed bugs at bay. Small cans or similar containers can be placed under each leg of the bed as was done in the nineteenth century. Nightly, the cans are filled with kerosene that will keep the bed bugs from crawling up the furniture.

of bed bugs are often signaled by a strongly disagreeable musky odor that is produced by the scent glands of the bed bugs, similar to the scent glands of stink bugs. Since they are nocturnal feeders, bed bugs hide during the day, between the box spring and mattress, between the wall and baseboard, or behind mirrors and pictures hanging near the bed.

Like other pests, bed bugs are introduced to well-groomed homes from another site of infestation. That could mean after a stay at a seedy hotel, unkempt motel, sketchy rooming house, communal dormitory, or a previously infested residence. Bed bugs, since they seek darkness during daylight hours, are easily transported in clothing, suitcases, bedding, stuffed toys, or furniture. Bed bugs might survive for extended periods of time without a meal, so that bargain-basement secondhand couch might well be the means by which a hungry batch of bed bugs could gain access into a squeaky clean, new apartment.

A heavy infestation of bed bugs should not be ignored, and professional assistance is recommended. The recent proliferation of bed bugs in urban centers has given rise to a whole new crop of entrepreneurs.

One of the most recent services offered incorporates bed bug–sniffing dogs. The dogs are trained to locate the bed bugs in places suspected of harboring infestations. Once the bed bugs have been located, elimination methods may proceed. Now that public consciousness has been raised about the rapid spread of bed bug infestations, there is a heightened sense of paranoia when an unknown creature is located in the home. Few things horrify a person more than finding an unknown bug in the bed. While bed bugs are a serious matter, most bugs found in the bed are benign creatures that happened to wander between the sheets accidentally.

HOUSE FLIES

So ubiquitous is the house fly, *Musca domestica*, and so closely it is adapted to life with humans, that it might deserve the title of the world's first domesticated animal, though in the case of the house fly, that title would carry considerably negative connotations. The house fly is found throughout the world, and it is never far from human habitation. Its habit of crawling through fecal matter, frequenting garbage cans and dumps, and alighting on dead and decaying animals ensures that it is an active vector for many human and animal diseases. It is a simple matter for the fly to transfer the germs it has picked up on its filthy forays onto the food that has just been laid out on the kitchen table. Face it: The house fly signifies filth.

Flies don't end their visit by merely eating and flying away. If there is anything tantalizingly decaying in the house or yard nearby, the house fly will soon lay eggs to ensure that a future generation will plague the hapless homeowner. Garbage left under the sink too long, a forgotten plate of putrefied meat, or a refuse receptacle too close to a doorway during a heat wave are all immensely attractive to the gravid female fly.

The hotter the weather, the less time it takes for an adult house fly to develop from maggots proliferating in decaying organic matter.

The Flyswatter

The house fly has the distinction of having its very own manu-factured device: the flyswatter, dedicated to the annihilation of arguably the most annoying pest to plague humankind. History has it that in the summer of 1905, while attending a baseball game in Kansas, Dr. Samuel Crumbine had a moment of enlightenment as he heard the crowd chanting "Swat the ball." Crumbine was a member of the Kansas board of health, and it was his personal mission to raise the public consciousness to the health threat posed by the house fly, which was enjoying a year of especial profusion and spreading typhoid. In a health bulletin that Crumbine published after the baseball game, he encouraged the people of Kansas to "swat the fly." Responding to Crumbine's call to action, a schoolteacher

named Frank H. Rose invented a fly bat, a contraption consisting of a piece of screen attached to a yardstick. The holes in the screen prevented the displacement of air that a solid object like a hand would cause, and without the change in pressure, the house fly could not detect the imminent doom that awaited it. Crumbine renamed the device a flyswatter. The flyswatter quickly gained popularity and today it can be found for sale at grocery stores, 99-cent stores, and novelty shops everywhere.

Cooking Cabbage Will Attract Flies

When you cook cabbage you must close all the windows and doors, or flies will get into the house. The aroma of cooking cabbage will announce to the neighbors that there is a large pot of *halupki*, or stuffed cabbage, on the stove as the aroma wafts through the neighborhood. A fly can find the tiniest hole in the window screen and gain entry to the kitchen, unlike the neighbor who must knock to get a savory treat. Once the fly has made its way inside, it will wait patiently on the water faucet or disguised on the floral tablecloth until it has the chance to zoom in and suck the juices from the wooden spoon. The fly is gifted with keen senses. It can detect the scent of cooking cabbage from great distances. The fly can see you approaching with the flyswatter from across the room. The fly will buzz off and disappear, hiding and awaiting the golden opportunity to deposit 200 eggs in the potato peels or cabbage core that is in the garbage pile. This is why it is necessary to take out the garbage every day.

Failure to take out the garbage may have dire consequences. Often when one takes a short vacation without taking out the garbage, the homemaker is greeted upon return by a swarm of flies buzzing in every window in the house. The sudden appearance of a large number of flies in the home is generally an indication that a mated female has found a food source hidden

in some forgotten darkened cove; it is not a sign of spontaneous generation, as was once believed.

> ### • A Brief List of • Fly-Borne Diseases
>
> Typhoid fever
> Cholera
> *Escherichia coli* (E. coli)
> Shigellosis
> Polio
> Diarrhea
> Anthrax
> Eye inflammation
> Tuberculosis
> Yaws
> Dysentery
> Trachoma
> Conjunctivitis
> Leprosy

Fruit Fly

Anyone who has ever left an overly ripe banana in the fruit bowl knows about the miraculous appearance of a swarm of fruit flies. Fruit flies in the genus *Drosophila* are also called vinegar flies and sour flies, and their olfactory senses are quite keen. Fruit flies are

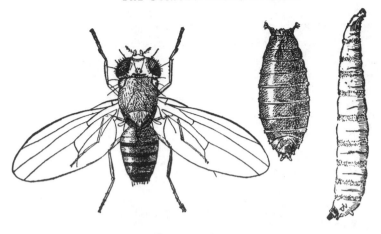

tiny, red-eyed, orange-bodied insects that resemble gnats.

A fruit fly is able to sense the presence of fermenting fruit from a considerable distance. The laboratory fruit fly that is used extensively in the study of genetics, *Drosophila melanogaster*, is frequently found in homes, orchards, and the produce section of grocery stores. Bartenders are well aware of the fruit fly's fondness for sweet liqueurs, and they are quite diligent to ensure that their establishments are not closed for health code violations should fruit flies be found dead in the bottles. While it may be difficult to eliminate the fruit fly from bars and restaurants with opened bottles of fruit-flavored

intoxicants, homeowners need only keep their house free from overly ripe fruit to prevent clouds of fruit flies from invading their kitchen.

SILVERFISH

Silverfish are under 1 inch in length. They are the bane of many a homeowner's existence. They are generally found in damp locations, like bathrooms and under the kitchen sink. Once they become established, they can become very difficult to eradicate. Silverfish feed on dry organic matter, and they are quite fond of starches, glues, and gum that are used in bookbinding and in the hanging of wallpaper. They may do considerable damage to a valuable book collection and because many old homes contain layer upon layer of wallpaper, there is an endless supply of food for this resourceful household intruder. If the basement has stacks of old newspapers and magazines, the homeowner has created a smorgasbord for silverfish. The diet of silverfish is not limited to paper products. They will also eagerly consume sugar, flour, breakfast cereals as well as their cardboard boxes, fabrics, and even insulation materials. Given enough time to proliferate, silverfish might eventually eat the entire home.

MULTICOLORED ASIAN LADY BEETLE

Everyone loves ladybugs, but there is one species, the multicolored Asian lady beetle,

Harmonia axyridis, that has become quite troublesome in many parts of North America. In the last years of the 20th century, reports began pouring in about invasions of ladybugs into people's homes at the onset of cold weather. Many of these beetles hibernate, but native species do not seek shelter inside homes. Infestations were so prevalent that homeowners needed to resort to vacuuming the beetles to get rid of them.

It is uncertain exactly how the multicolored Asian lady beetles entered North America. Most lady beetles are predatory, and their primary diet consists of aphids and other similar insects that are significant agricultural pests. Native beetles are often collected from areas where they hibernate and then released into orchards and other areas where there is a need for biological control of pest insects.

There is evidence that as early as 1916, the U.S. Department of Agriculture released multicolored Asian lady beetles in California to help control the pecan aphid. They were released again in California in 1964 and 1965. Between 1978 and 1982, multicolored Asian lady beetles were introduced to the states of Connecticut, Delaware, Georgia, Louisiana, Maine, Maryland, Mississippi, Ohio, Pennsylvania, and Washington. There is no evidence that those regulated releases resulted in a naturalized population of these beetles, but it isn't difficult to imagine that possibility. In 1988, a population of wild Asian beetles was discovered north of New Orleans, the result of an accidental introduction from a freighter; this population quickly spread through the eastern United States. Reports of home invasions of massive quantities of multicolored Asian lady beetles began occurring in the 1990s.

Since the beetles feed on pests that are found on trees,

homes in wooded areas are especially prone to invasion. In Asia, the multicolored Asian lady beetles seek shelter from the winter cold in cracks and crevices of cliffs, but lacking those geographic features in many areas of North America, they have adapted to seeking shelter indoors. Tall buildings and structures with contrasting light and dark areas are most attractive to the beetles, and they congregate outside in sunny locations as the weather begins to cool. These migrations toward shelter generally begin on warm sunny days after the first cold snap, traditionally the time of year known as Indian summer. Following their natural inclinations to overwinter in the cracks and crevices of rock formations, they find ingress to the homes through cracks in their foundations, around windows and doors, and in areas with poor weatherproofing like attics and basements. Once indoors, they congregate into large masses inside walls, in dark corners of the cellar, and in isolated areas of the attic. Mild sunny days will cause the multicolored lady beetles to become active, and at that time they may begin to fly and possibly enter the living quarters, where they are immediately noticed. They will also make an appearance in the spring as they congregate near windows in an attempt to get outdoors.

As long as they are in secluded areas of the home, the lady beetles go unnoticed, but once they become more active, they become troublesome. If disturbed, the multicolored Asian lady beetles will secrete a yellow body fluid that is actually their blood. This fluid has an unpleasant odor, and it will stain walls and fabrics. For this reason, it is best not to swat the beetles, but to use other methods of removal. Using a vacuum cleaner is a brilliant means for removing the beetles, but keep them out of the bag. A nylon stocking can be rubber-banded to the vacuum hose. With the stocking in place, the beetles can be sucked into the bag it forms when drawn into the hose; the bugs can then be released outdoors far from the

home. The captured beetles can also be stored until spring and released after their desire to hibernate has passed. If the beetles are to be kept, it is necessary to supply them with some moisture and to keep them in a covered container with numerous airholes. The best place to locate the container is in a protected, unheated area like a porch or garage.

BOXELDER BUGS

Multicolored Asian lady beetles are not the only black-and-red insect species that forms large groupings (known as aggregations) and seeks shelter from winter by moving into homes. The native eastern boxelder bug, *Boisea trivittata*, is similarly predisposed. The eastern boxelder bug, a scentless plant bug, is found throughout most of North America east of the Rocky Mountains.

Numerous homeowners have written to WhatsThatBug.com with inquiries about the aggregations of black-and-red insects that congregate on warm sunny walls in the cool fall weather. These aggregations may contain tens of thousands of individual boxelder bugs. Because of these aggregations, which often occur in the late summer during political rallies, boxelder bugs are called Democrat Bugs, Populist bugs, or politician bugs in the Midwest because their large numbers reminded people of the participants at political gatherings. Boxelder bugs often enter homes as cool weather arrives since the homes are choice sites for hibernation.

Despite their large numbers and the annoyance that boxelder bugs cause fussy homeowners, they are benign insects that feed on the seeds of the boxelder and related maple trees and do not cause any damage to the plant itself.

The eastern boxelder bug is slightly more than ½ inch in length. It has a red body, and its wings are black with red markings. When wingless nymphs gather with mature adults, they almost appear to be two different species, which to the uninformed observer may resemble a political rally with opposing parties wearing different colors.

While aggregations of boxelder bugs in yards are likely to cause nothing more than an aroused curiosity, the insects have an annoying habit of seeking shelter indoors as the weather begins to cool. Large numbers of eastern boxelder bugs manage to enter houses through small cracks in the structure and around the windows and doors, and when they appear in significant numbers, they present a harmless nuisance. Vacuuming the insects in the same way as was explained for the multicolored Asian lady beetle (page 147) is the best means of ridding the home of the unwanted bugs.

6

HOUSEHOLD VISITORS

Friendly Houseguests

IT PAINS ME greatly when WhatsThatBug.com receives images of smashed house centipedes, swatted dobsonflies, or mangled tailless whipscorpions. Thus I created the "Unnecessary Carnage" section of the website in an attempt to educate the public on the benefits of allowing some insects to cohabit with us. Insects are frequently prone to senseless slaughter, be it from an overzealous homeowner who doesn't want to see bugs, from a strapping he-man who is a closet arachnophobe, or from a youngster who fears the unknown.

Many creatures discovered in the home are benign or even beneficial insects and arthropods that have accidentally entered through doors and windows. They might want nothing more than to find their way back outside, yet their startling appearance often results in their meeting an untimely end by a frightened human. There are some creatures that seek shelter indoors during inclement weather, but other than being an annoyance, they will do no harm. Other creatures are commonly associated with human habitation, but they are beneficial predators that will help to rid the home of other unwanted invaders. It is important to distinguish these creatures from the true problem species identified in the previous chapter. Once I wrote to a woman that nothing short of an atomic bomb would eliminate all insects from her yard in an attempt to make her realize that many insects are our friends.

PSEUDOSCORPION

Because of its tiny size and its disproportionately large front pinchers, the pseudoscorpion is sometimes mistaken for a tick. The pseudoscorpion is a harmless predatory arachnid less than ¼ inch in length. Unlike its related namesake, it does not contain any venom. Pseudo-scorpions are found the world over, and their outdoor habitat includes leaf litter, the bark of trees, spaces under stones, and the interiors of caves. Perhaps their natural proclivity for caves causes them to frequent dwellings, where their unusual scorpion-like appearance may cause the homeowner some alarm. Pseudoscorpions never grow large, will not threaten humans or pets, and will not damage the home or its

furnishings. Any other unwelcome insect visitors, however, have cause to fear because this effective predator is capable of capturing and eating significantly larger prey, including house flies and cockroaches.

MASKED HUNTER

Immature masked hunters attract attention in the home because of a very unusual anatomical characteristic of the immature insect. The body of the masked hunter nymph is covered with a sticky surface that attracts all manner of lint, dust, sand, and debris, acting as a camouflage coating that effectively masks the insect by allowing it to blend with its surroundings. The layperson often describes the masked hunter as a lint bug. I once received a photo of a masked hunter nymph that was bright blue because the carpet in the home where it was found was composed of blue fibers. Masked hunters are assassin bugs, and they are very efficient predators that might bite if they are carelessly handled. Masked hunters are often called masked bed bug hunters because they will feed ravenously on the blood-sucking scourge that has been spreading through many urban areas. Though I hesitate to recommend letting nature take its course when it comes to doing battle with bed bugs, I would lobby for the preservation of any masked hunters that are found inside the home in the hope that if any bed bugs are present, they will quickly be dispatched by this curious predator.

HOUSE CENTIPEDE

Of all the creatures found inside the home that can be considered perfectly harmless and enormously beneficial, none seems to attract more attention, to cause more hysteria, and to conjure more exaggerated descriptions than the house centipede, *Scutigera coleoptrata*. House centipedes are outdoor predators that also seem perfectly adapted, in fact comfortable, sharing your

home. They are nocturnal hunters, and they are rarely encountered during the daylight hours, which they pass in dark, damp areas like under the sink, in the basement, in the bathroom, or in crawl spaces. Outdoors, they may be found in garages, woodpiles, under rocks, and in similar sheltered places. But, come darkness, the house centipede begins to prowl about in search of prey, including cockroaches, flies, moths, bed bugs, crickets, silverfish, earwigs, and small spiders, many of the creatures that home-owners would rather not encounter indoors.

It is during these nocturnal ramblings that the house centipede is noticed. Sometimes

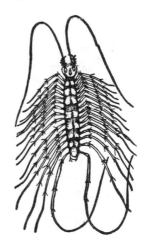

a house centipede is seen darting across the carpeted floor while the human inhabitants are watching television. Sometimes a light is snapped on in the kitchen during a midnight refrigerator raid, revealing a house centipede hunting on the kitchen wall. A trip to the bathroom in the middle of the night might reveal this long-legged predator searching for food in the shower. House centipedes are often found in sinks and bathtubs where they have become trapped if they cannot scale the slippery sides to flee the rising sun.

The house centipede is a creature graced with amazing mobility. Its rapid darting locomotion is aided by the 15 pairs of legs, far short of the 100 legs implied by its name. The legs of the house centipede are considerably longer than the legs of most centipedes, and they move in an undulating motion that defies description. The body of a house centipede is less than 1½ inches in length, but the length of the legs and antennae, and the rapidity with which it moves, creates the illusion of a

much larger creature. Like other members of its class, house centipedes have fangs and venom, but it is generally believed that the fangs of the house centipede are incapable of breaking human skin, and the venom is not toxic to people. Despite its frightening and often startling appearance, the house centipede is considered to be not only perfectly harmless but actually quite beneficial in that it rids the homes of other unwanted visitors. House centipedes do not leave cobwebs lying about like spiders do. Since they hide during the day and are rarely seen, it stands to reason that house centipedes should be not merely tolerated, but welcomed into the home since their benefits far outweigh an occasional frightening encounter.

A Letter from the What's That Bug? Archives: The Creatures

This letter was one of the first I ever received back in 2000. I had a tough time convincing the querent that "The Creatures" really were house centipedes.

Hello Bug Person,

I saw your site and thought maybe you could help me and my roommate out. We have creatures. That's what we call them, because they are unlike anything we've ever seen. In the last three places we've lived, we have seen the Creatures in our basement. They are similar to centipedes in that they are long, have many legs, and are creepy. But that's where the similarities end. Centipedes are flattened with legs that look like this ^ with one joint, but these Creatures have 2 joints, like spider legs. They don't have as many as a centipede but definitely more than 8. The legs are generally the same size too, not different lengths like a house centipede. They don't have the front "fangs" like a centipede but a mandible similar to a spider's—no antennae, no little butt feelers. And they come in 3 different colors. I've seen very large ones (4–5 inches), black with white spots; others were just as big but dark brown; and just the other day, in our new duplex, we found a little one maybe 2–3 inches long and light brown. They are very fast and I even hit one with a book, cutting off its lower half, and the rest of it got away. Yeah, these things are evil. Nobody knows what these things are. We've had hunters, Floridians, Arizonians, and other self-proclaimed bug experts, but we always get the same thing: a hideous blank stare and lonely nights in our basement. Can you tell me what the creatures are?

• The Christmas Tree and Preying Mantises •

People who bring a live Christmas tree into the home often awake finding more than just presents under the tree. If a Preying Mantis ootheca, or egg case, was present, the warm indoor conditions may cause the young mantises to hatch prematurely, and they will be found swarming in the branches. Numerous other insects may also be introduced to the home on a living tree.

SOME HOUSEHOLD SPIDERS

Some spiders accidentally find themselves indoors, and other species are perfectly content spending their entire lives inside our comfortable homes, reproducing generation after generation without ever setting foot outside. The world, it seems, can be divided into people who love and tolerate spiders, and the arachnophobes who irrationally fear all spiders. While I fall into the former category and never kill a spider in the house, going so far as to let them spin their webs where they please, I would never attempt to convert those who fear spiders into arachnophiles. I hope to at least foster an understanding of this fascinating group of predators.

Very few spiders are actually poisonous enough to present a problem for humans. Though all spiders contain venom, the bite of most species will do little more than cause a local reaction that quickly dissipates. Exceptions in North America are the black widow and her relatives, the brown recluse, and possibly the hobo spider. Of the three, the glossy black widow with her red hourglass is the most distinctive. Black widows are found inside homes occasionally, but they generally prefer to live outdoors in crawl spaces, garages, sheds, and in woodpiles. The black widow is nocturnal, hiding during the day in some crack or crevice on the periphery of the sheltered area she has chosen for her webs. She does not wander, but will remain in her web in the same location month after month, making it possible for one to know where she lives and to

respect her, giving her distance. It is only the female black widow that bites, and the minuscule male is rarely if ever noticed.

One of the most commonly encountered spiders in the home is the harmless long-bodied cellar spider, *Pholcus phalangioides*. This spider has a tiny body and very long legs, and it builds a feeble nest often in the corners of rooms and in basements. The long-bodied cellar spider, also known as a cobweb spider, has an interesting habit of gyrating its web wildly when it is disturbed.

The common house spider,

Parasteatoda tepidariorum, is another domestic species rarely found far from human dwellings. It is found worldwide, and it tends to spin its messy webs in corners of rooms and dark areas. The spider is rather nondescript, with a vague spotted appearance. They are not aggressive, do not wander, do not leave their webs, and will feed on flies and other household intruders that might be troublesome. Tolerating the common house spider in the home has its benefits.

Cream house spiders or long-legged sac spiders in the genus *Cheiracanthium* are common visitors inside, but they are not quite as benign as the two previous species. Cream house spiders are a pale yellow color, and they often build sacklike webs indoors. The spider will wander about more than other house spiders, and its long jaws enable it to bite, though the bite is not particularly dangerous. People who want to rid their home of these spiders but do not want to kill them can easily relocate the bugs using the martini glass method described below.

• Martini Glass Trap •

Often insects that find themselves trapped in the home would like nothing better than to regain their freedom. Wasps and spiders are generally harmless unless they are mishandled. Unwitting household intruders batter themselves against window glass in their efforts to get outside; the best thing you can do is assist them in getting there. One of the easiest and safest methods for relocating insects trapped in the home is with an empty martini glass. Simply capture the insect in the vessel portion of the glass while holding on to the stem. Then slide a postcard between the window and the glass's rim, and you can safely move the disoriented insect back into the yard.

TAILLESS WHIPSCORPION

Though they are normally encountered in tropical countries, residents of the southern states occasionally find a frightening, but harmless, tailless whipscorpion in their home. These spiderlike creatures have claws like scorpions and whiplike front legs, and they scuttle sideways like a crab. They are shy, nocturnal hunters that will feed on any cockroaches that they encounter in their nightly forays. Since they lack venom, other than their ability to startle, they are perfectly benign creatures that are frequently victims of unnecessary carnage.

WESTERN CONIFER SEED BUG

Had it remained confined to its native Pacific Northwest range, the western conifer seed bug, *Leptoglossus occidentalis*, would never have made our list of household visitors. During the 1970s, however, individuals were noticed in the eastern portions of North America, thousands of miles from their home territory. These introductions were probably due to human assistance, though the exact source of the accidental establishment cannot be ascertained. The western conifer seed bug found the climate in the eastern part of the continent to its liking; because there was a readily available food source, the species multiplied. Both adult and immature western conifer seed bugs feed on the sap of resin-rich green pinecones and occasionally the twigs and needles of many species of conifers, so they do little damage to the trees themselves, though they do have a negative effect on the developing cones, which wither and fall off the tree.

The western conifer seed bug is now very well established across North America, everywhere but the southern and Gulf states. In the very late 20th century and into the early 21st century, reports of sightings in many European countries were confirmed, doubtless due to the importation of stacks of lumber that may have contained hibernating adults.

The western conifer seed bug can be recognized both by its dull orange-and-brown coloration and by its long antennae. Its most distinguishing feature though is a widening on the hind leg that gives the family members the shared common name of leaf-footed bug or big-legged bug. Since homeowners are often prone to swatting this relatively large intruder should it be encountered inside, this action releases what some find to be an offensive odor, and what others have described as the scent of apples, the smell of

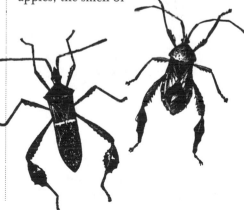

grass, or the odor of pine. Because of the scent, the western conifer seed bug is sometimes mistaken for a stink bug, though the odor released by the latter is rarely described as pleasant.

Because of their habit of entering homes to seek shelter from the winter cold, western conifer seed bugs gain attention in the autumn along with some true stink bugs like the brown marmorated stink bug. None of these species poses any threat to humans, pets, or homes. They will not breed indoors, and they will not bite. Because they are just seeking shelter from the elements, if they escape notice upon entering, they will find a secluded place and rest until the warm sunny days of spring arrive. At that time, they again attract attention as they seek egress at the bright windows.

WHAT'S THAT LIVING IN THE AQUARIUM?

While the aquarium isn't commonly thought of as a location for household insects, most authorities on tropical fish dedicate a section of their book to insects that might threaten tropical fish. Sometimes parasitic worms may be introduced with live food that is preferred by certain tropical fish. Freshwater aquarists who purchase live plants for a more natural habitat may unwittingly introduce immature aquatic insects that will grow and thrive in the home aquarium. Probably the likeliest introductions are dragonfly or damselfly naiads, and water tigers, the immature form of aquatic beetles. While insects large enough to do harm to adult fish are difficult to miss, a younger predator could quickly wipe out a school of newly hatched fish fry.

LEAVING ON THE PORCH LIGHT AT NIGHT

Homeowners often wonder why that large beetle or moth has entered their home, and the insect's appearance is sometimes accompanied by paranoid

delusions that an assault or infestation is immanent.

Numerous nocturnal insects are attracted to electric lights, and keeping the porch light on at night and then opening the door is a sure way to invite an otherwise outdoor creature into the comforts of the domicile.

Moths are among the most visible insects that are attracted to porch lights. Giant silk moths, which may attain a wingspan of 6 inches in North American species and nearly twice that size in some tropical species, are frequently attracted to porch lights. In North America, luna moths, Polyphemus moths, and cecropia moths are sometimes found on the walls near the light source. Sphinx moths or hawkmoths—including the great poplar sphinx, the Pandora sphinx, and the striped morning sphinx—often visit the home if the porch light beckons. Tiger moths, underwings, plume moths, and a host of other smaller and more insignificant species are frequently discovered the following morning.

Many beetles are attracted to lights, including the familiar June bug or May beetle. Other related scarabs like the eastern Hercules beetle, North America's heaviest beetle, are attracted to lights, as are the spectacularly noble stag beetles. Many of the longhorned borer beetles like the sawyers in the genus *Prionus* are found near artificial light sources, and should they ever enter a home, they are sure to generate fear and loathing in some individuals and wonder and curiosity in others. Click beetles like the eyed elater and countless other smaller families of beetles also find themselves drawn irresistibly to electrical beacons lit by those who avoid the dark.

The giant water bug or toe-biter has such a predictable reputation for the allure of artificial illumination that it also goes by the common name of electric light bug. Giant water bugs are the largest of the true bugs, and they are sure to startle any observer upon an initial encounter. There are countless reports available of prodigious numbers of electric light bugs circling stadium lights and illuminated parking lots, especially in areas near swamps and lakes where the giant water bugs prefer to hunt. Though they are not aggressive, the electric light bug will not hesitate to bite if it is carelessly handled.

Other insects that are frequently encountered at porch lights include lacewings, katydids, preying mantids, mayflies, and the impressively grotesque or gorgeous (depending on the eye of the beholder) dobsonfly. Finally, many a homeowner has reported an opportunistic orb weaver

spider constructing a web near a lamp that is lit at night so it can take advantage of the flying nighttime denizens that are attracted to the lure of nocturnal illumination.

CAMEL CRICKETS

Though they are not especially problematic, many homeowners are appalled at the discovery of a significant population of large hopping creatures with long antennae that have taken up residence in the cool and dark basement. Often, a colorful verbal description is enough to identify the camel cricket or cave cricket in the tongue-twisting family Rhaphidophoridae. These humpbacked creatures are able to hop several feet; snapping on a light causes them to jump about as they scatter and seek darkened hiding places, creating a quite startling effect. A clean, dry home is not a conducive environment for camel crickets, but since most basements are dank, dark places used to store items that should otherwise be discarded, many homes harbor a population of them. Should they be discovered and should they be intolerable, the best means of removing the crickets is to make the basement less desirable real estate. Clear out piles of wood,

stacks of newspaper, rolled carpeting, and boxes of clothing, and the camel crickets will no longer feed and breed. The scary appearance of the camel cricket belies its shy and harmless nature.

SPRINGTAILS

Springtails have been known to be the cause of chagrin for countless homeowners when they appear in great numbers in unwanted places. While they are

benign creatures, springtails can become a nuisance when they proliferate in the shower, under the kitchen sink, in the basement, and in other damp places in the home. Even the most fanatically clean homeowner can become flummoxed when thousands of springtails begin hopping about in the shower. Because they are found in damp locations where mold is also found, springtails may actually be beneficial since they will consume the mold that is beyond the reach of the cleaning arm.

LAWN SHRIMP

Also known as house hoppers, lawn shrimp are not insects, but terrestrial amphipods, a group of crustaceans. Lawn shrimp are native to Australia, but they have been introduced to California, Florida, New Zealand, and the British Isles, where they happily live in the well-watered landscaping under the ever-present ivy and other ground covers, feeding on dead organic

What Crawled Out of the Firewood?

Households with wood-burning stoves or fireplaces often have an indoor area for storing wood. Numerous insects, including many beetles, have larvae that bore in wood. The indoor warmth speeds up the metamorphosis, and causes the emergence of adult insects. Among the most common insects to emerge from firewood are longhorned borer beetles and jewel beetles. These insects may also emerge from milled lumber many years after the wood has been finished.

matter in the soil. They need to be kept moist, but too much water causes them to drown. They are shrimplike in appearance, and they move by hopping great distances. They are unobtrusive gray creatures about ⅓ inch long while living in the yard, but when the first heavy rains of the year occur, they flee the flooded outdoors and seek the drier interiors of homes and garages, where they die in great numbers, turning pink or orange, like cooked shrimp. They cannot survive in the dry indoor environment. Their sudden appearance does

bring out the curiosity in homeowners, who are startled by the invasion, a sign that there is probably too much watering of the garden since lawn shrimp need constant moisture to survive. The best way to reduce their numbers, especially in southern California, is to reduce the frequency of watering the landscape.

BESS BEETLE FOUND IN MAN'S LUNG

Sometimes even friendly buggy visitors can create a problem if they are in the wrong place at the wrong time. A benign Australian Bess beetle was reportedly removed from a man's lung, where it was lodged after it crawled into his breathing stoma. The 74-year-old man had been diagnosed with lung cancer 12 years earlier, and he had a permanent breathing stoma. Doctors suspected his cancer had returned since he entered the hospital complaining of a scratching feeling in his chest. X-rays revealed a beetle nearly 1½ inches long in his collapsed lung. Bess beetles, or passalid beetles, are generally found in rotted wood, and it was learned that the day before the man first noticed the symptoms, he had been removing trees with a chain saw. It is suspected that the beetle entered the house in his shirt, and later sought a dark hiding place by entering the open tracheostomy, crawling down to the main bronchial passage. The patient was later advised to cover his stoma while asleep to prevent a similar occurrence.

7

WEATHER WONDERS

How Insects Are Affected by
Various Climactic Conditions

BRIGHT, SUNNY, warm summer days are often literally buzzing with life. Butterflies flit about from flower to flower, and honeybees gather nectar. Crickets sing, and cicadas buzz from the treetops. Everywhere you look, insects may be found. There is no disputing that summer is the peak time for insect life, especially since so many bugs have such a short life span, but not all insects are active while the sun is shining, or when the nights are warm. Unlike humans whose schedules are regulated by such artificial points of reference such as beginning the workweek on Monday, ironing clothes on Tuesday, and eating spaghetti on Thursday, insects' schedules are governed by natural phenomena, including precipitation, barometric pressure, and the length of the daylight portion of a day.

SIGHTING CALENDAR FOR OHIO

January: Snow scorpionflies are found meandering on freshly fallen snow.

February: Snow stoneflies are sighted congregating on bridges near streams.

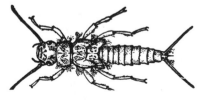

March: Mourning cloak butterflies are found flying over patches of snow in the wooded areas.

April: Bright green six-spotted tiger beetles hunt for prey on paths and sidewalks.

May: Luna moths are sighted by lucky night owls.

June: Fireflies light up at night, thrilling children on summer vacation.

July: Dobsonflies attracted to lights frighten porch sitters.

August: While building nests in the ground that are provisioned with paralyzed cicadas, cicada killers dive-bomb humans who have ventured outside.

September: Hickory horned devils leave the trees to pupate underground.

October: Large preying mantids hunt for flying insects on goldenrod.

November: Western conifer seed bugs seek shelter inside homes.

December: Cecropia moth cocoons may be found attached to tree branches.

INSECTS IN THE SNOW

Insect life seems to be able to adapt to the most adverse conditions. In many parts of the world, winter is cold and there is snow on the ground, and this is not typically thought of as a time when teeming insect life can be found. However, there are some species that are uniquely adapted to cold weather.

A Butterfly in the Winter

The mourning cloak is a large purplish black butterfly with yellow wing edges and a row of blue spots. The undersides of the wings resemble dried leaves, allowing this butterfly to blend

in with forest debris when it alights. The mourning cloak is often the first butterfly of the year that is seen in the Northern Hemisphere around the world. Someone tramping through the woods on a sunny day in January when there is still snow on the ground in Russia, Europe, or Canada might be startled to see a large, dark butterfly flying about. Dark colors absorb heat, and the morning cloak commonly spreads its wings and aligns its body to take advantage of the feeble rays of the winter sun to warm its body so that it has the energy to fly.

At first, it might seem puzzling because there are no flowers on which the mourning cloak might feed. It is generally believed that all butterflies feed on the nectar from flowers, but some species have adapted to taking nourishment from other sources. The mourning cloak is one of those, and it will readily feed on rotting fruit, though that is also in short supply in the woods during January. The first warm days of winter trigger the rise of sap in trees, and the sweet, sticky substance can be found oozing from wounds on trunks and branches everywhere in the woods. This sap constitutes the primary diet of the mourning cloak when there is nothing else to be found while the forests are blanketed with snow.

The life cycle of the mourning cloak easily explains its seemingly unseasonable appearance. Adult mourning cloaks mate in the waning days of winter after hibernating in hollow trees, rocky crevasses, and—in modern times— unheated buildings. Though they appear when there is snow on the ground, they do not fly during blizzards. It's the warmth of the sun that rouses them from winter slumber. Survival is always a key factor for any insect, and the instinct to survive should help explain this seemingly aberrant behavior. There are fewer predators to feed on the developing caterpillars if the insect gets an early start, and there are also fewer competitors for the tender leaves sprouting from barren branches with the coming of spring.

After mating, the female mourning cloak seeks the first sprouts on the branches of willow trees, and there she lays her eggs. Elm and certain other trees will suffice, but pussy willows, a harbinger of spring, are among the earliest of plants to sprout across the range of the mourning cloak. Once the eggs hatch, the caterpillars, also known as the spiny elm caterpillars, quickly develop. In England, the mourning cloak is known as the Camberwell beauty.

Snow Fleas

Snow fleas are not true fleas, and they will not bite your pets. Snow fleas are actually a type of springtail, a group of wingless primitive insects in the order Collembola. Many people believe that springtails are the most numerous insects on the planet, with up to 250 million individuals per acre. They have a cosmopolitan distribution, and they have adapted to a wide range of conditions, including living on the surface of tide pools, swimming pools, and on the surface of the snow.

Springtails get their name because many members in the order have a forked organ called a furcula, which is normally folded and locked in place under the abdomen. When the springtail extends the furcula, the contact with the ground catapults the insect into the air, allowing it to jump a significant distance. They are unable to control their hopping with much accuracy, so if a group of springtails is startled into activity, they will chaotically hop about willy-nilly in every direction. Springtails are often mistaken for fleas due to their means of locomotion and their minute dimension, with most members of the order measuring a minuscule $\frac{1}{16}$ inch in length.

Though they are found in the winter, snow fleas are not active during snowy, frigid weather.

They hibernate in leaf litter under a deep blanket of snow, but on warm and sunny winter days when patches of snow melt, often near the trunks of trees, the snow fleas are stimulated into becoming active. They appear like specks of pepper, hopping about on the surface of the snow. They feed on decaying plant material, bacteria, fungi, algae, pollen, microscopic creatures, and sap.

Currently, scientists are researching a protein found in springtails that acts like antifreeze, preventing ice crystals from forming in the body cells, which would otherwise rupture in subzero temperatures. It is hoped that these studies will lead to the better preservation of body organs for transplantation, since lower temperatures could be used without fear of ice crystal formation.

Three Different Snow Flies

There are three completely unrelated insects that are commonly called snow flies. One of them, a wingless crane fly, is a true fly. This snow fly, also called the snow crane fly, is found in the winter months in North America, where it can be found crawling sluggishly on the surface of fresh snow in temperatures as low as 14°F. The life history of these 1/3-inch-long spiderlike creatures is still largely a mystery, though there is believed to be some association with the nests of small mammals like mice and chipmunks. The snow crane fly is found from the arctic tundra to as far south as the Appalachian Mountains.

The second snow fly is the snow scorpionfly, and there are family representatives known from Tasmania and from the northernmost regions of North America. The snow scorpionfly is commonly found walking on the surface of the snow in the middle of winter. The body temperature of this fly depends on the absorption of short-wave and long-wave radiation rather than on the surrounding temperatures. Neither the temperature of the snow nor the surrounding air temperature affects the body temperature of the snow scorpionfly. The radiation is dissipated slowly because the fly inhabits the boundary layer of the snow where the conductance of heat is low. There is information indicating that holding a snow scorpionfly in the hand will cause it to die, presumably from overheating, as the delicate balance of its typical radiation absorption has been upset. Snow scorpionflies feed on the exposed leafy parts of mosses and liverworts that stay green all winter.

The third snow fly is actually a member of a family of winter stoneflies that range over much of North America. The aquatic naiads are found in streams under rocks and gravel, where they feed on aquatic plant material, and the adults, which feed on blue-green algae, are most commonly found on snow or resting on bridges near streams. Beginning in late January or early February, the nymphs leave the water and metamorphose into adults. The appearance of the adults, though they are found on the snow, is an indication that winter is nearing an end. The metamorphosis is likely triggered not by a change in temperature, but by the lengthening of the hours of daylight after the winter solstice. Adult winter stoneflies are black or dark brown insects about ½ inch long, and some are winged while other species are wingless. Of the three insects commonly called snow flies, the winter stoneflies are the largest. Adults are short-lived, dying soon after mating.

Finding Cocoons and Egg Cases in the Winter

Though they are theoretically not active during the winter, the observant naturalist often takes advantage of the lack of foliage in the winter months to locate the overwintering pupae of the giant silk moths and egg cases of certain insects. Many caterpillars overwinter by pupating underground, or they are buried in leaf debris under the snow, but there are several distinctive cocoons that may be found still attached to tree branches. The caterpillars spin their cocoons out of dense silken fibers that help insulate the dormant pupae during the winter freeze.

The Prometheus moth or spicebush silk moth constructs its cocoon within a leaf that is secured to the branch with silk. Trees that sustained a healthy population of caterpillars often have many of these slender cocoons hanging from their branches. From a distance they resemble dried leaves that refused to be dislodged in the winter winds, but on closer inspection their true identities are revealed. The cocoon of the closely related tulip tree silk moth is very similar in appearance.

The large cocoon of the cecropia moth may be found fastened lengthwise to a stem or branch of the host plant. Occasionally, a leaf is incorporated into the spinning of the cocoon, though it is generally fashioned without any

additional support material. The cecropia moth has an ingenious method of providing egress for the adult moth from its cocoon. A series of valves, one on the pointed top of the outer layer, and a second at the end of the denser inner layer, allow the moth to exit without undue hardship or causing the tattering of its wings. The closely related Columbia silk moth makes a very similar cocoon.

The emperor moth, which ranges throughout much of Europe and Asia, is the only giant silk moth found in the British Isles. The cocoon is described as sturdy, coarse, thin-walled, and pear-shaped, and it is spun up among tree leaves that remain attached to the branches during the winter months.

The egg cases or ootheca of preying mantids are often noticed clinging to the upright branches of shrubs once the leaves drop. These frothy masses are occasionally mistaken for cocoons, but rather than hatching a single moth, several hundred baby mantids will emerge.

SIGHTING CALENDAR FOR CALIFORNIA

January: The large winter mosquito, which rarely bites humans, will lay its eggs in stagnant water of birdbaths and containers that catch rainwater.

February: Desert spider beetles with their small heads and inflated abdomens are often found in desert areas.

March: Impressive swarms of painted ladies fly north from Mexico each year in the spring. Some years the numbers are so low as to escape notice, whereas in other years hundreds of butterflies may pass by each minute.

April: Population explosions of white lined sphinx caterpillars appear periodically when there is lush desert vegetation after a wet winter.

May: Tall clouds of water midges are often seen near water and they may be so numerous as to appear to be smoke.

June: Beautiful banded alder borers are sometimes attracted to fumes when homeowners apply a fresh coat of paint.

July: California root borers, with their wondrous antennae, startle campers because they are attracted to lanterns and campfires.

August: Tarantula hawks visit milkweed blossoms for nectar and fly low over sandy ground in search of tarantulas, especially in desert regions.

September: Though they may be found all year long, potato bug sightings often peak in the autumn.

October: Painted tiger moths (*Arachnis*) are attracted to porch lights, where they often lay clusters of eggs.

November: Male California trapdoor spiders become active with the first rains and search for mates, often falling into swimming pools.

December: Spiny nymphs of the keeled treehopper often infest tomato plants that are still growing in the garden.

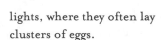

FIRE BUGS:
INSECTS AND BRUSH FIRES

Though it has been observed often that moths are attracted to flames only to perish in the fire, and this is repeatedly used as a metaphor for self-destructive behavior, there are insects that are attracted to fires as a means to perpetuate the species. When a brush fire or forest fire occurs, creatures that cannot flee or seek shelter perish, including numerous insects. There is a relatively well-documented forest regeneration process, and there are some plants that require the heat of a fire before their seeds will germinate. Once the new plant growth begins, animal life also returns, but in a bizarre reversal of the norm, there are certain insects that are actually attracted to burning brush fires. Insects that are attracted to fires are known as pyrophilic, or fire-loving, species.

There is a bean-size species of jewel beetle, or metallic wood borer beetle, found in the western portion of North America that is known by the descriptive names of fire chaser beetle and fire beetle. The beetle is attracted to heat and smoke, and it often arrives at a burn site before the flames recede, occasionally flying in the faces of firefighters and landing on their bodies. These beetles are also attracted to fires on a smaller scale, including burning trees and stumps, oil fires, burning refuse dumps, barbecue fires, and even the smoke from cigarettes.

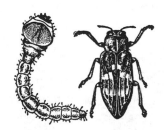

Though it took considerable research, in the 1960s a scientist discovered that the insects have infrared heat receptors that enable them to identify a potential fire from as far as 30 miles away. The species *Melanophila acuminata* was the subject of that research, but other members of the genus exhibit similar heat-seeking behavior. Since there will not be a likely habitat for a new brood at these locations, it is most likely that the oil fires and barbecues are false alarms for the fire chaser beetles that prefer to lay their eggs under the bark of freshly charred wood. These wood-boring beetles rarely lay eggs on healthy trees since a healthy tree is generally resistant to attack. The fire chaser beetles depend on dying trees to provide a food source for their young, and fire is not the only means by which a tree becomes stressed. It would seem, however, that a freshly burned area, though not the only source for stressed and dying trees, would definitely provide an ample food supply.

Australia, another region prone to regular brush fires, has its own species of fire beetle, *Merimna atrata*, also a member of the jewel beetle family of wood-boring beetles. Like its New World cousin, the Australian fire beetle, a larger insect nearly 1 inch long, is attracted to forest fires because its larvae develop in freshly burned wood. At dawn and dusk, Australian fire beetles swarm to fires. The beetles then pair up and mate, and the female lays her eggs under the bark of seared trees, ensuring a future generation.

A species of rhinoceros beetle called the triceratops beetle is found in the southeastern United States, and it might be the only insect to earn the distinction of being a pyromaniac. There are reports of triceratops beetles flying down chimneys while fires are burning, and then spreading around the embers, causing cabin fires. It is presumed the beetles were attracted to the smoke. Like the previously mentioned beetles, this behavior may be linked to laying eggs in dead and decaying wood, which breaks down more easily after being charred.

Not all fire bugs are beetles. There is a living fossil known as the incense cedar wasp that has remained unchanged since Mesozoic times, 251 million years ago. Living fossils that have not evolved over time are relatively rare, and they are unusual in that not only have they remained unchanged but they have survived major extinctions that have killed off most of their coevals. The incense cedar wasp is the only living representative of its family, and it occupies a unique niche within the balance of nature of its particular habitat. This wasp, *Syntexis libocedrii*, is rarely seen except by firefighters. It lays its eggs deep in the sapwood of fire-scorched trees from California north to British Columbia. It is reported that the cedars and junipers that provide food for the young are often still smoldering when the female lays her eggs. Like the previously mentioned beetles, the larvae are wood-boring,

grublike creatures that aid in the decomposition of organic material by breaking down dead wood and returning its component compounds to the soil.

Smoke flies in the family Platypezidae are also attracted to burn sites. They arrive shortly after the fire, and they may also be attracted to campfires. The smoke fly larvae feed on fungus that grows on wood that has been burned, and represen-tatives of the family are known from North America and Australia, especially in high fire zones. Their attraction to burn sites is well documented on both continents.

Some flat bugs in the family Aradidae are also attracted to recently burned, forested areas. Flat bugs live under bark and feed on fungus, and the conditions after a fire favor the growth of the fungus they eat. Unlike the previously mentioned fire bugs, flat bugs do not arrive while the fires are still burning, but their occurrence shortly afterward warrants classifying them as insects that are attracted to fire and smoke.

SIGHTING CALENDAR FOR FLORIDA

Because of its climate, many Floridian species are not limited to specific seasons and can be found all year, though sightings are often more common during certain months.

January: The beautiful green gaudy sphinx moth is often attracted to lights during the winter months.

February: The polka-dot wasp moth, which mimics a stinging insect, and its caterpillar, the oleander caterpillar, are both found all year long in Florida, though reports in February are especially numerous.

March: With his long exaggerated antennae, the male southern pine sawyer is attracted to lights that are left on at night near coniferous forests.

April: The male rainbow scarab with his long, curved horn and coppery red and green metallic coloration is a lovely dung beetle.

May: Distasteful to predators, the huge, colorful, flightless eastern lubber grasshoppers are most common in the spring, but may be found all year long. They will spread their rudimentary wings, hiss, and secrete a smelly fluid if they are threatened.

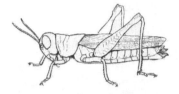

June: The eyed elater is a click beetle with prominent eyespots that can flip itself over by clicking its jointed body against the ground. It is most often seen in the summer months.

July: The gigantic female golden silk spider or banana spider makes a large, strong web of golden silk, and there may be one or more tiny males a 50th of her size sharing the web with her.

August: The beautiful four-spotted spider wasp may be found taking nectar from flowers and paralyzing spiders to feed her brood.

September: The large green darner dragonfly cruises the airspace above marshy habitats in search of mosquitoes and other flying prey.

October: Visible all year long in the South, but most common in the fall, the giant swallowtail and its caterpillar, the orange dog, may be found wherever citrus grows.

November: The male green orchid bee, a tropical species that became established in Florida in the early 21st century, uses chemical compounds derived from orchids to attract a mate.

December: If a mating female musk mare, or twostriped walkingstick, and her smaller partner are disturbed, they may spray a noxious chemical with startling accuracy directly into the eyes of the perceived threat.

INSECTS AND THE WIND

Especially for flying insects, the wind, be it a gale force blast or a softly blowing breeze, may aid in species distribution. Inhabitants in hurricane-prone areas often report strange insects after a storm, and it is not unusual for tropical and subtropical species to be buffeted far from their native habitats. They may survive for short periods of time in foreign lands, but rarely will these hitchhikers on the wind become established. Either their food is not readily available in the new location, or the climate is not conducive to their survival, so their days are numbered. There are cases though in which new species have become established, most often in Florida or Texas, after an accidental introduction that might be a result of a hurricane.

Though it cannot be conclusively proven, there is some indication that the green orchid bee that was observed initially in Florida in 2003 may have been transported by a hurricane. A tropical species that typically ranges in the Caribbean parts of Central America and Mexico, this lovely metallic green bee has become a fixture in the southern portions of Florida where the climate and availability of cultivated flowers suits its needs.

Butterfly Migrations Aided by the Wind

In Los Angeles, they are the Santa Ana winds and in Spain they are the Sirocco, but whatever the name, they are devil winds. Devil winds blow hot off of the sands, and they

bring with them many winged creatures, including painted lady butterflies. Though their migrations are not as predictable as the annual migrations of the monarch butterfly, the painted lady butterflies, which range throughout the Northern Hemisphere, are subject to intermittent migrations that can be quite spectacular, especially at the beginning of the spring Santa Ana winds, when thousands of individuals fly low to the ground each hour.

The altitude at which they fly enables them to take advantage of the wind while exerting a certain amount of control over the direction they travel by making a partial compensation for wind drift. There is considerable evidence that population explosions of painted ladies occur after el niño rains trigger lush green plant growth in arid desert regions of Mexico and northern Africa. The plants feed the caterpillars that often leave nothing green for a future generation. Once the caterpillars mature into flying adults, they ride the desert winds north, away from their place of birth, to disperse in areas where there is a fresh food source. Irregular migration patterns like this coupled with the wide variety of available food plants help ensure species survival by reintroducing individuals to areas where local populations may have died off because of famine.

How the Wind Affects the Flights of Moths

When the winds begin to blow, it is a sure bet that moths will appear. Winds bring about changes in temperature, humidity, and precipitation, and these changes trigger metamorphosis in the moths. A moth that has overwintered in a cocoon may be awaiting the spring rains to emerge and transform into a winged creature of the night whose goal is to mate and produce a new generation, and the winds help these moths travel to distant lands. Many moths migrate. The silver Y moth from the United Kingdom annually flies south to Africa in nocturnal swarms on

seasonal winds. The silver Y moths, though they rely on the winds for speed, do have some ability to control the direction in which they migrate; otherwise, they might be blown off course and be left to die if dropped at destinations with unsuitable conditions for survival. Moths may influence their direction and speed of movement in several ways. They are known to migrate only on nights when wind directions are broadly favorable, meaning that they are blowing from north to south. The moths select their altitude so that they stay high, where the winds are the fastest, ensuring that they will arrive as quickly as possible. They also fly in a roughly downwind direction, which adds their own flight speed to the wind speed, taking advantage of the tailwind. The moths are able to make adjustments when the wind direction is off target, partially compensating for wind drift. While it is known that the silver Y moth is capable of these aerodynamic feats, the exact means behind the ability is still a mystery.

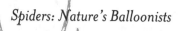

Spiders: Nature's Balloonists

The young of many orb weaver spiders depend on the gentle spring breeze to help with species distribution. Once the egg sac hatches, hundreds of predatory spiderlings are released. If all the spiderlings remained in the same location, there would be enormous casualties due to cannibalism. The spiders have adapted an ingenious method to circumvent the young feeding on one another. After hatching, the spiderlings seek an area of higher elevation, climbing a tree or wall, and waiting until they feel a light wind. With the onset of the breeze, the spiderlings begin to release a strand of silk that catches on the breeze, billowing out away from the perch. The spiderlings use a favorable wind to balloon away, dispersing the brood to numerous new homes far away from one another and the negative ramifications of extreme sibling rivalry.

SIGHTING CALENDAR FOR TEXAS

January: Milkweed assassin bugs, which may be seen all year-round in Texas, can be located as they stalk prey in the garden.

February: The first white lined sphinx moths of the season may be mistaken for hummingbirds as they feed from flowers at dawn and dusk.

March: The first Polyphemus moth sightings for the year often come from Texas in the early spring.

April: Fiery searchers hunt for caterpillars in trees and along the ground.

May: Toe-biters in great numbers are attracted to brightly lit parking lots near swampy areas.

THE CURIOUS WORLD OF BUGS

June: Enormous horned eastern male Hercules beetles battle over nesting sights near rotting cavities of oak trees.

July: Boldly patterned, black-and-white cottonwood borers with long antennae gather to feed, mate, and reproduce near poplars and willows.

August: Black witch moths, fleeing the summer rains in Mexico, migrate north and seek shelter in the eaves of houses when the sun rises.

September: The gigantic Belzebul bee-eater feeds on bees and wasps in meadows and open areas.

October: With the coglike projection on its back, North America's largest assassin bug, the wheel bug, is often described as looking like a prehistoric dinosaur as it hunts for prey in the garden.

November: Mature male angle-winged katydids call to their mates from trees and shrubs.

December: Some gray bird grasshoppers are able to survive through the winter, reproducing in the spring, so it is possible to see adults of this species at any time of the year.

LOOK WHAT CAME OUT WITH THE RAIN!

If all the insects whose appearances were predicated on rain were profiled here, this book would be endless. Termites swarm, butterflies emerge from chrysalides, beetles metamorphose into adults and search for mates, and moths are attracted to porch lights left on at night. What follows are some of the more interesting examples of insects and their relatives whose

182

biological clocks are triggered by precipitation.

While the eensy-weensy spider of nursery rhyme fame had an unfavorable experience with a sudden downpour, not all spiders find a generous shower to be problematic. The first rains of the season seem to trigger wanderlust in the male California trapdoor spider. The male spider has a leg span of up to 2½ inches, and may be recognized by his shiny black legs and orange or tan abdomen. Females have larger heavier bodies and shorter legs and they rarely leave the burrow, which is equipped with a hinged door for ambushing prey as well as providing a protective cover to the lair. The male's long legs assist him in his search for a mate, as he often wanders far from his original burrow while on his mating quest. Sadly, numerous wandering male California trapdoor spiders end their quest unsuccessfully because of the potential obstacles that get in their way. Falling prey to other predatory animals, tumbling into swimming pools and drowning,

and a host of other life-threatening challenges face the male spider once he leaves the safety of the burrow that has been his home for such a long time. As spiders go, California trapdoor spiders are long-lived, with females often living through several seasons. Males are reported to have a lower life expectancy, in part because of the high mortality rate involved in wandering in search of a mate. In captivity, California trapdoor spiders have been known to live up to 8 years.

Velvet mites are large, red, fuzzy, spiderlike creatures that emerge in great numbers in arid regions after rains. Velvet mites, or angelitos as they are sometimes called, attract attention because of their bright coloration and relatively large size, reaching well over ¼ inch in length. Velvet mites wander about searching for food. The immature stages are often parasitic on grasshoppers while the adults prey on termites and eat insect eggs. Since both grasshoppers and termites react to the rainy season as well, the days following a rain are an ideal

THE CURIOUS WORLD OF BUGS

hunting season for velvet mites. Much of the biology of velvet mites remains a mystery. Adults are subterranean dwellers for most of the year, and they crawl to the surface for only a few hours to hunt in the days after the rain.

The Fascinating Life of the Rain Beetle

The life cycle of beetles in the family Pleocomidae is so intricately tied to precipitation patterns that they have the unique distinction of earning their common name *rain beetles* from their activities after autumn and winter rains. Rain beetles have a limited range along the western coast of North America from northern Baja California, Mexico, north to southern Washington, and nowhere else. According to the latest taxonomy, the group contains a single genus, *Pleocoma*, and 34 species. The ranges of the individual species are often quite limited, and they are determined by geographic barriers characteristic of the mountainous terrain.

With the onset of the autumn

and winter rains, adult rain beetles that have been waiting underground for the precipitation for months emerge simultaneously from their burrows. They have lived underground as larvae, feeding on the roots of oaks and conifers for between 10 and 13 years, making them among the insects with the greatest longevity. They may have metamorphosed from the pupa to the adult form several months earlier, but without the rains, they wait. Female rain beetles are flightless, and male rain beetles have a bumblingly erratic flight similar to that of the June beetles that they superficially resemble. Adult rain beetles do not feed. The atrophied mandibles do not function, and the esophagus is sealed. The short life of the adult is sustained by the fat that accumulated during the decade plus life spent as a subterranean grub.

The female rain beetle digs her way to the surface when the rain begins and releases her enticing scent, a pheromone that has been described as vaguely lemony by observers in the field. The male rain beetle flies low over the ground at twilight, in the waning light of dusk and again in the moments before sunrise, trying to follow the female's alluring smell. Once he hones in on her, the two retreat to a nuptial chamber she has prepared, and they mate. The male soon dies, and the female seals the opening and digs as deeply as 6 feet under before laying her eggs. The female then dies as well. Upon hatching, the larvae repeat the cycle by feeding on roots for 10 or more years.

Lower-elevation species of rain beetles often require the ground to be saturated by a soaking of several inches of rain before emergence, while higher elevation species may begin to fly minutes after the start of the season's first storm. It is unclear if it is the moisture itself or the change in barometric pressure or some other factor related to the rain that is the force that triggers the mating behavior of the adult rain beetles.

Since the female rain beetles do not fly, there can be only limited species distribution. This would explain how numerous species evolved when individual populations became isolated from one another. This may also be the key to the mass emergence, which in some species of rain beetles is limited to a single day. Having all potential reproductive adults present at the same instant in time will increase the odds that males will find a mate and perpetuate the species.

SIGHTING CALENDAR FOR AUSTRALIA

January: Numerous species of cicadas loudly serenade mates from the treetops throughout the summer down under.

February: Fiddler beetles, large, brown scarab beetles with unusual green or yellow markings, have reached the end of their season, and they will begin to disappear until next summer.

March: March flies, which are often called horse flies in other parts of the world, often bite

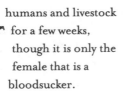

humans and livestock for a few weeks, though it is only the female that is a bloodsucker.

April: Beautiful, colorful black Jezebel butterflies can be found taking nectar from flowers in the eastern coastal region of Australia.

May: Spitfires, defoliating sawfly larvae that are often mistaken for caterpillars, feed in groups on eucalyptus leaves. When disturbed, they collectively wiggle their tails and expel a nasty brown fluid from their mouths.

June: Common crow butterflies overwinter in large aggregations, going dormant until warmer weather arrives.

July: The giant burrowing cockroach or rhinoceros cockroach, the world's heaviest cockroach, is sometimes found aboveground, though it typically burrows as deep as 3 feet below the surface.

August: House centipedes that have adapted to living inside homes are occasionally noticed as

they scurry about the floors at night in search of prey, including cockroaches and spiders.

September: Mole crickets occasionally suspend their subterranean excavations long enough to surface and startle folks with their unusual lobsterlike bodies and digging front feet.

October: Named for the somewhat greasy appearance of the semitransparent forewings, the big greasy butterflies, also known as clear-wing swallowtails, may be found mating and taking nectar from bottlebrush flowers.

November: Aggregations of adults and immature, small-headed bronze orange bugs congregate on citrus trees, sucking the sap from tender young branches.

December: Gaily colored Christmas beetles, a group of scarab beetles, begin their annual appearance in time for the holidays.

8

MAKING MONEY WITH BUGS

PROFITING FROM INSECTS is most often thought of in the negative context of extermination. Toxic products for pest control that pollute the planet are readily available at every grocery store. Using paranoid ad campaigns, extermination companies will separate you from your hard-earned money by offering a schedule of chemical warfare and a sense of false security. Agricultural pests have a definite negative effect on the profit margins of many farms and orchards. Subsequently pesticide industries contribute positively to the gross national product while poisoning the environment.

Rating systems in restaurants have brought vermin like cockroaches in commercial eateries to the forefront of public awareness, and the elimination of the pests and the return to a good grade have ensured the solvency of the exterminator. Without insects, life as we know it on our planet would surely cease to exist.

Children have an innate curiosity about bugs, and fostering this interest will lead to a greater appreciation of the wonders of nature. It is also possible to pursue an insect-related career that is both ecology and economy friendly. This chapter focuses on some of the positive

BEEKEEPING, OR APICULTURE

There is little doubt that the single most important contribution insects have made to the economy is beekeeping, or apiculture. While the production of honey is the most obvious commercial product produced by honeybees, beeswax is another significant product of beekeeping. In recent years, with the increasingly higher profile of holistic medicine, bee pollen and royal jelly have become top-dollar medicinal supplements.

There is rich archaeological evidence of the domestication of bees dating back several thousands of years. The oldest known surviving hives were discovered in 2007 at an Iron Age site at Tel Rehov in Israel. This nearly 3,000-year-old apiary contains between 75 and 200 hives, and it is estimated that it could have held more than

ways that insects can contribute to the economy because it is actually possible to make money with bugs.

a million bees, with an annual yield of 1,100 pounds of honey and 155 pounds of beeswax. The unique site contains a full apiary and demonstrates a large-scale operation. Though the site in Israel represents the oldest site that has been discovered, there is older evidence of beekeeping in ancient cultures. Carvings that depict beekeeping dating back 4,500 years appear on the walls of a temple in Egypt. The carvings illustrate men removing honeycombs from cylindrical hives that resemble the hives discovered in Israel. Other carvings at the site have been interpreted to suggest the separation of honey from the beeswax. Sealed pots of honey were discovered in the more than 3,000-year-old tomb of King Tutankhamun, and the honey is still viable. This would indicate that honey has a longer shelf life than any other known food.

A cave painting discovered at the turn of the 20th century in the Cave of the Spider (*Cueve de la Araña*) in Valencia, Spain, dated to between 8,000 and 15,000 years ago, represents the oldest known record of man using

honey. Recorded in red paint on the walls of the cave is a lone figure climbing several vines to remove honey from a wild hive. Nearby, large bees are flying about. The figure is known as the Man of Bicorp. It is believed that prehistoric man may have already discovered that smoke will pacify the bees, enabling the removal of the honey without the risk of stings.

There is a written history of beekeeping attributed to Aristotle in ancient Greece, dating to at least 300 BC. Ancient Greek coins from Ephesus in Turkey contain representations of bees, documenting the importance of these insects to the people of the time. Most coins contained the visage of the current ruler, and getting an

image on a coin is a big deal. This could be evidence of the value of the ancient honey trade among the Greeks. Ancient Romans also have a rich written history of beekeeping, dating as far back as the first years of the common era.

Before the invention of the modern movable frame hive, honeybees were kept in hollow logs, wooden boxes, ceramic pots, and woven straw baskets. Harvesting the honey meant destroying the hive along with the young bees and the queen. Advancements in the 18th century led to scientific observations of the honeybee hives and the invention of the box hive by Francis Huber of Switzerland. The Huber hive, though mobile, had fixed, solid frames that did not facilitate easy honeycomb removal. In the 19th century, an American named Lorenzo Langstroth invented the first movable frame beehive, which was patented in 1852. Finally, the honeycomb could be removed without destroying the hive.

The mobile hives also added to the potential income available to the beekeeper. Certain crops, notably almonds, but also apples, peaches, and avocados, depend greatly on honeybees for fertilization. If no hives were near the orchards, there could be no fruit production. The mobility of modern hives allows the boxes to be moved to the fields and orchards where they are most needed. Modern beekeepers often ship their hives across the country on trucks where they are most needed during the blossoming season of the crops.

In 2001, the world honey production was 1,392,000 tons, with Asia and Europe producing the most honey

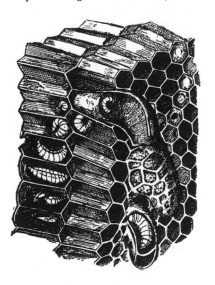

by continent. The greatest honey-producing countries in 2005 were China, Argentina, Turkey, Ukraine, and the United States. The United States consumes more than twice the amount of honey it produces.

There are many studies that indicate that consuming local honey produced by honeybees that take nectar from local flowers significantly reduces allergies in individuals who are sensitive to pollen. The surge in the number of farmers' markets has provided venues for beekeepers to sell their honey to local consumers. I buy my own local honey from Aunt Willie at the Atwater Village Farmers' Market in Los Angeles. According to Aunt Willie, local honey is anti-inflammatory, helps dissolve mucus, will relieve a sore throat, helps control hay fever, stimulates healing of sores (including those caused by diabetes), relieves arthritis, and calms an upset stomach.

The benefits of bee pollen are also considerable. Bee pollen is a natural anti-inflammatory, helps control hay fever, aids digestion and reduces appetite, improves concentration, increases sexual stamina, reduces the effects of stress, builds red blood cells, is beneficial for the prostate, and is good for bodybuilding. Royal jelly, according to Aunt Willie, in addition to many of the previous benefits, also enhances mental functions, helps fight anxiety and depression, eases menopausal symptoms, helps fight osteoporosis, has antiaging properties, is beneficial to skin and hair, and has antimicrobial properties. Human civilization's benefits from honeybees are truly legion.

Colony Collapse Disorder

Disease among domesticated honeybees in not a new phenomenon, and various mites, microbes, and pathogens have been responsible for hive loss for years. In 2006, however, a new syndrome manifested where the workers in a hive would mysteriously vanish without a trace. Often bee larvae and pupae were left in the hive untended, and honey and pollen were present. There are numerous theories as to the cause of colony collapse disorder (CCD), but there is no

• Grandma's Cough Syrup •

The medicinal qualities of all three of the following ingredients are undisputed. Combined and taken in moderation, this cough syrup tastes better than any available commercial product.

- 1 part honey
- 1 part lemon juice
- 1 part bourbon or whiskey

Combine and warm so the honey incorporates with the other ingredients. Will last indefinitely in a bottle without refrigeration. Take a tablespoon several times a day as needed.

conclusive proof. It is entirely possible that multiple factors are contributing to CCD, including mites, microbes, pathogens, pesticides, genetically modified crops, migratory beekeeping (in which hives are transported great distances), climate change, and even electromagnetic radiation from cellular telephone towers. Despite there being no known cause for the disorder, the syndrome is having a significant negative impact on the production of honey and the pollination of crops that depend on the honeybees for pollination, including almonds.

SILKWORMS AND SERICULTURE

The second-biggest insect-oriented economic industry in the world is undoubtedly the production of silk, or sericulture. The discovery that the silkworm, *Bombyx mori*, could

be used to create fabric is credited to Lei-tzu, the wife of the famous Chinese emperor Huang-ti, in the year 2640 BC.

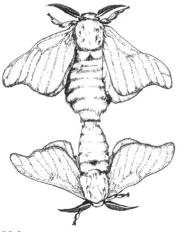

Voluminous ancient writings credit Lei-tzu with the cultivation of the mulberry tree on which the caterpillars feed, rearing of the worms, reeling of the silk, and the invention of the loom. Lei-tzu was honored with the title of Goddess of the Silkworms, or *Si-ling*, upon her death. After centuries of domestication, the silkworm has been selectively bred to produce the finest silk, and unnecessary

characteristics, including the ability to fly, have been lost. Because it is virtually flightless, unlike the honeybee, the domestic silkworm is a true domesticated insect that is incapable of survival on its own in the wild.

The production of silk was a closely guarded secret in China, and it took nearly 3,000 years before the process was exported to Japan, with the assistance of some Koreans. At about the same time, around AD 300, the industry was begun in India. Persia and eventually Greece and Rome were exposed to the production of silk, first by trading in the finished textiles and then through the acquisition, via smuggling, of the eggs of the silkworm and the seeds of the mulberry trees. Silk trade traveled from China to the Mediterranean along the famous Silk Road. Silk fever spread through the rest of Europe, and silkworms were brought to Virginia in 1613. In 1619, the first silk was produced in the colony. Though silk production was attempted numerous times through the early 20th century

in America, the experiments inevitably led to failure.

Silk is a fibrous substance produced by numerous insects and spiders, but it is the silk of only the domesticated silkworm that has any economic significance. Insects use silk to construct cocoons, make nests, and weave webs. The silk of the domestic silkworm is unique in that the caterpillar spins its cocoon from a continuous filament between 800 and 1,200 yards long. To harvest this filament, the pupa must be killed with steam or fumigation while still in the cocoon, because upon emergence after metamorphosis, the adult moth produces a substance that dissolves the cocoon. Emergence of the adult cuts and tangles the filament of the cocoon. The cocoons are softened in hot water, which releases the filament, enabling it to be reeled. Filaments from multiple cocoons are reeled together producing yarn, and the number of cocoons determines the gauge of the thread. It takes about 5,000 silkworms to make a single silk kimono.

Silk is known as the fabric of kings, and before the introduction of synthetic materials, its use in the 20th century was primarily for women's hosiery and fine garments, though during the war years, parachutes were made from silk. Even with the introduction of synthetic materials, there continues to be a desire for silk in modern garments and upholstery fabrics. China is once again the top producer of the fiber. In 2005, China produced 54 percent of the world's silk, followed by India with 14 percent.

A Gossamer Shawl Woven from Spider Silk

Though it may never become economically feasible to harvest the silk from spiders, in 2009 an 11-foot-long shawl, woven from the silk of over 1 million golden silk spiders from Madagascar, was put on display at the American Museum of Natural History in New York. The saffron-colored silk is six

times stronger than steel, and the webs are so strong the spiders are able to snare small birds that become entangled in the orbs.

PREDATORY INSECTS SOLD TO GARDENERS

The interest in pesticide-free, organic gardening has resulted in a flourishing business of selling natural predators over the Internet or at local nurseries. Lady beetles or ladybugs have been sold for decades to control aphid populations, and there is some degree of controversy regarding the collection of wild hibernating convergent lady beetles to be sold to the naive public. The harvesting process will reduce the numbers of wild beetles in their original habitat, potentially threatening the existence of the species. The release of the convergent lady beetles to areas where they are not native may reduce the populations of native predatory lady beetles. Releasing adult convergent lady beetles invariably causes them to fly away, providing little or no benefit to the well-intentioned gardener.

Green lacewings that are available as adults, larvae, and eggs might be a smarter choice for the home gardener who wants to control insect pests. Both adults and larvae will consume a wide variety of pests, including small caterpillars, whiteflies, mites, scale, thrips, psyllids, and mealybugs, and they are most effective with aphids. Adult lacewings have wings, though they are feeble fliers, and there is not much chance that they will fly away like ladybugs are prone to do. The larvae, which are known as aphidlions, are very effective predators.

Minute pirate bugs in the genus *Orius* are not as readily available as the previously mentioned predators, but they are especially effective in the control of thrips and other small insects. Immature nymphs

and winged adults have the same feeding habits. Minute pirate bugs are also effective predators in greenhouses.

There are several suppliers that sell predatory mites to help control specific problems in the garden and greenhouse. Mites in the genus *Hypoaspis* will help control soil-inhabiting insects, mites, springtails, and the larva of the fungus gnat. Mites in the genus *Amblyseius* can be used to control thrips on the leaves of garden plants.

The egg cases or oothecae of preying mantids have also been available for insect control for decades. The advantage to using these egg cases is that, once they hatch, the young will stay close because they don't have wings. Young mantids will eat aphids, fruit flies, and other small insects, and the size of the prey will increase with the size of the predator.

FOOD FOR PETS

People have a penchant for their pets, and there has been a growing interest in exotic cold-blooded pets for many years now. Tarantulas, scorpions, frogs, and lizards are all commonly available in pet stores today, including the larger chain stores. Those pets need to eat, and the result has been a need for suppliers of crickets, mealworms, and fruit flies for all local pet stores. People that need to buy live insects for their pets also become regular clients at the pet stores since they need to replenish their food supplies on a weekly basis. The dollars

that are generated by the sale of live insect food for pets has a significant positive effect on the world's economy. The suppliers, distributors, and retailers are all profiting from this niche industry.

BUTTERFLIES RELEASED AT WEDDINGS, OTHER JOYOUS OCCASIONS, AND FUNERALS

Butterflies represent change and transition in many cultures and to many individuals, and it is logical that they should come to symbolize many of life's rites of passage. Entrepreneurs recognized the potential for profit, and the last decade has witnessed the growth of a new industry. There are numerous companies that supply live butterflies—such as monarchs, painted ladies, red admirals, Gulf fritillaries, and giant swallowtails—for release at private and public events

throughout the United States. There is an increasingly vocal group of experts, including Jeffrey Glassberg (president of the North American Butterfly Association), Robert Robbins (curator of Lepidoptera at the Smithsonian Institution), James Tuttle (president of the Lepidopterists' Society), and noted authors Paul Opler and Robert M. Pyle, who oppose this practice because of negative environmental effects to native butterfly populations. The actual business websites cite their own experts in support of the practice, and promote the preservation of the rain forest fauna and claims of no negative ramifications to the environment that can be traced to the release of captive specimens.

Potential clients should read both viewpoints before making a decision.

INSECTS AS DECORATIVE ITEMS

Because of their jewel-like beauty, many butterflies and moths have been incorporated into jewelry and other decorative items. There is a long history, traceable to Victorian England, of using butterflies and beetles to create decorative collages. Beginning in about the 1930s, pieces of morpho butterfly wings were set into jewelry to create necklaces, earrings, bracelets, and cuff links. Often this butterfly wing jewelry was sold in souvenir shops and was painted with tropical scenes that included sunsets and palm trees. Coasters for drinks, serving trays, and small framed pictures were also quite common at the time. While these items may still be found in antiques shops and swap meets, there is a modern industry that is still going strong. The jewelry of today often includes insects and arachnids embedded in Lucite and fashioned into earrings, key chains, and belt buckles. Framed collections of gorgeous butterflies and exotic insects can be found in souvenir shops and through Internet distributors. The business of insects as decorative items is flourishing.

BUTTERFLY PAVILIONS

At zoos and botanical gardens, butterfly pavilions are springing up around the world. These venues, which often charge an admission separate from the rest of the museum, are generally seasonal, depending on the climate. Several times a week they are restocked with newly metamorphosed butterflies and occasionally large moths that have been raised to maturity from purchased pupae. Visitors in the butterfly pavilions can stroll in gardens while hundreds of colorful butterflies flutter about, visiting the flowers or specially placed dispensaries of sugar water, and landing on people with brightly colored clothing. A decade ago, butterfly pavilions were relatively rare, but now most large cities boast one somewhere near, and residents from around the country can travel but a short distance to enjoy the winged beauty of tropical and local butterflies in a contained environment.

Butterfly Farms

Because of other relatively new industries like butterfly pavilions, butterflies for decorative purposes, and butterflies that are released at events, there grew a need for places to raise the stock that was required. In places where the climate is conducive, farms for raising this new form of livestock began to proliferate. Many butterfly farms are open to the public for tours for a nominal fee.

EDIBLE INSECTS

Television shows like *Fear Factor* brought eating spiders, grubs, and various other insects, each selected to be more visually gross than the last, into the public consciousness. The contestants are dared to put unthinkable things into their mouths and then chew and swallow to earn cash rewards. In actuality, there are numerous cultures in which eating insects is a common practice. *Entomophagy* is the technical term for the practice of eating insects as food. Thailand and Mexico are two countries where consumption of insects is routine, and there are regions in North America, Central America, South America, Africa, Asia, the Middle East, Australia, and New Zealand where eating insects is common-place for indigenous people. The practice seems to have eluded Europeans and Western culture until relatively recently. Though actual citations are proving elusive at the moment, I can recall chocolate-covered ants being a novelty item during the early 1960s.

The insects that are most frequently consumed worldwide are crickets, cicadas, grasshoppers, ants, various beetle grubs, caterpillars and pupa of large moths, larvae and pupae of bees and wasps, termites, and scorpions and tarantulas. There are distinct advantages to eating insects. They are high in protein and high in healthy fat. Insects are also high in vitamins and minerals. Insects can be raised for food consumption, and the cost of producing food from traditional livestock is much greater than the more efficient cost of raising insects.

Thailand is one country where a variety of deep-fried insects are sold on the streets by vendors. One of the insects consumed is the giant water bug or toe-biter, which is considered a real delicacy. Giant water bugs are available packaged at some Thai grocery stores in North America, and some Thai restaurants even serve them on the menu stateside. Other deep-fried Thai delicacies include cicadas, locusts, mantids, crickets, and grasshoppers. Ants, termites, caterpillars, pupae, and beetle grubs are also steamed, barbecued, ground, and prepared in other manners.

Grasshoppers (which are

· Roasted Crickets, Oaxacan Style ·

A plate of roasted crickets will make for quite a conversation piece at your next party. Live crickets suitable for human consumption may be purchased from most local pet stores, where they are sold to feed reptiles, amphibians, tarantulas, and scorpions. Crickets must be roasted alive, but they will hop away if they are not prepared properly. If the crickets are chilled first, they will not hop when placed on the cookie sheet. Preheat the oven to 200°F, and arrange the chilled crickets in a single layer. Roast for about 1 hour until they are crunchy, but not burned. Toward the end of roasting, they may be seasoned with freshly squeezed lemon juice and salt, but make sure the crickets are completely dry before storing. Store in an airtight container or, better yet, eat immediately.

called chapulines), crickets, and queen leaf-cutter ants are all consumed in Mexico, most commonly in Oaxacan cuisine where the indigenous Indian culture heavily influences the food preparation. Roasted crickets are a common snack available at our favorite Oaxacan restaurant in Los Angeles, Guelaquetza on 8th Street.

American Indians, especially those living in the western states, regularly ate, and in some cases continue to eat, certain insects. Mormon crickets, which are known to swarm some years and threaten crops, are a popular roasted food. Certain fly larvae and caterpillars, including the white lined sphinx and Pandora moth (called piuga) are collected and eaten. Grasshoppers are probably the most commonly eaten insects among Native Americans.

Eating insects is a viable means of helping control their populations. A swarm of locusts of biblical proportions may decimate a grain crop, but rather than fretting that there is no food left to eat, enterprising survivors should probably just turn to the plague for nourishment. Locusts are grasshoppers, and grasshoppers have been identified as one of the more nutritious insects consumed around the globe.

Before determining that you would never, ever eat an insect, it would be prudent to consider the possibilities of accidental ingestion. The proverbial fly in the soup, worm in the apple, or the deep-fried cockroach with the French fries from the fast-food restaurant might seem like obvious, easily avoidable situations, but you probably unknowingly eat insects on a daily basis. Processed foods invariably contain insects that do not get separated from the grains and produce that are ground, canned, or bottled in manufacturing plants. The maximum levels for insect contamination allowed by the U.S. Food and Drug Administration take that inevitability into consideration. Canned corn, orange juice, chocolate, peanut butter, flour, frozen vegetables, hops used in beer, and ground spices all have legal permissible limits for insects or insect parts that find their way into the finished product purchased by the consumer.

Eating insects is a practice that is growing in popularity, and there are numerous websites that offer such treats as chocolate-covered ants, chocolate-covered crickets, roasted crickets, and scorpions imbedded in lollipops, though these items sell at gourmet prices. Eating insects is still considered to be a novelty in Western culture, and only the bravest gourmand will attempt the act. As our population continues to grow, and as our food supply continues to diminish, the time may come when we are forced to rely on insects for sustenance.

SOME ENTERTAINING INSECT-THEMED MOVIES

Insects have served as a source of inspiration for numerous film directors. Most often they are used to horrify and repel the viewer, but on occasion they may serve as comic relief, to metaphorically represent the human condition, and sometimes to inspire awe through their beauty and diversity. I now present a drastically edited list of some of my personal favorites:

Angels and Insects directed by Phillip Haas (Playhouse International Pictures, Samuel Goldwyn Company, 1995). Victorian England provides the setting for this adult-themed love story between a penniless entomologist, whose collection of Amazonian insects was lost in a shipwreck, and the daughter of an aristocrat.

Hairspray directed by John Waters (New Line Cinema, 1988). The world's biggest buggy dance competition pits Ricki Lake, who dances "The Bug," against Amber Von Tussle, who dances "The Roach," in racially tense 1962-era Baltimore.

The Invasion of the Bee Girls directed by Denis Sanders (Centaur, 1973). A beautiful female scientist experimenting with bees is transformed into an oversexed mutant murderess with compound eyes.

Microcosmos directed by Claude Nuridsany and Marie Perennou (Miramax, 1996). Spectacular close-up photography and minimal narration make this investigation of the overlooked invertebrate life in a French country meadow a stunning viewing experience.

Mimic directed by Guillermo del Toro (Miramax, 1997). Mutant cockroaches impersonating human beings attack subway passengers and scientists in New York City.

Naked Lunch directed by David Cronenberg (20th-Century Fox, 1991). Loosely based on the writings and life of author William S. Burroughs, *Naked Lunch* follows the life of an insect exterminator who discovers that the insecticide he is using has hallucinogenic powers.

Phenomenon (released in the United States as *Creepers*) directed by Dario Argento (Titanus and New Line Cinema, 1985). A psychotic killer on the loose in the Swiss countryside may have met his match with a young schoolgirl who can telepathically communicate with insects.

Them directed by Douglas Gordon (Warner Bros., 1954). Atomic testing in the New Mexico desert produces a colony of giant ants that are destroyed, but not until mated queen flies take off to start a new colony in the Los Angeles River Basin.

References

BOOKS

Borror, Donald J., and Dwight M. DeLong. *An Introduction to the Study of Insects*. New York: Holt, Rinehart and Winston, 1971.

Bulfinch, Thomas. *Bulfinch's Mythology*, New York: Avenel Books, 1979.

Comstock, John Henry. *An Introduction to Entomology*. Ithaca, NY: Comstock Publishing Company, 1947.

Comstock, John Henry, and Anna Botsford Comstock. *A Manual of the Study of Insects*. Ithaca, NY: Comstock Publishing Company, 1926.

Eaton, Eric R., and Kenn Kaufman. *Kaufman Field Guide to Insects of North America*. New York: Houghton Mifflin, 2007.

Gertsch, Willis J. *American Spiders*. Princeton, NJ: D. Van Nostrand Company, 1949.

Hogue, Charles L. *Insects of the Los Angeles Basin*. Los Angeles: Natural History Museum of Los Angeles County, 1993.

Howard, Leland O. *The Insect Book*. Garden City, NY: Doubleday, Doran & Company, 1937.

Innes, William T. *Exotic Aquarium Fishes*. Philadelphia: Innes Publishing, 1938.

Johnson, Kurt, and Steve Coates. *Nabokov's Blues*. Cambridge, MA: Zoland Books, 1999.

Lutz, Frank E. *Field Book of Insects*. New York: G. P. Putnam's Sons, 1948.

Nabokov, Vladimir. *Ada or Ardor: A Family Chronicle*. New York: McGraw-Hill, 1969.

REFERENCES

Nabokov, Vladimir. *Pale Fire.* New York: G. P. Putnam's Sons, 1962.

Reitsma, Ella. *Maria Sibylla Merian and Daughters.* Los Angeles: Getty Publications, 2008.

JOURNAL ARTICLES

White, Michael James Denham. "The Chromosomes of the Parthenogenetic Mantid Brunneria Borealis." *Evolution* 2 (1948).

SELECTED WEBSITES

Appel, Alfred. Nabokov's Interview: www.kulichki.com/moshkow/NABOKOW/Inter15.txt

Book of Insect Records: http://entnemdept.ufl.edu/walker/ufbir

Brisbane Insects and Spiders: www.brisbaneinsects.com

BugGuide: http://bugguide.net/node/view/15740

Cicada Mania: www.cicadamania.com/cicadas

Curwen, Thomas. *Los Angeles Times.* "The Case of the Shadowy Beetle." http://articles.latimes.com/2009/may/18/local/me-beetles18

Discover Life: www.discoverlife.org

Encyclopedia Britannica: www.britannica.com

Eric Eaton: http://bugeric.blogspot.com

Kennedy, Randy. *New York Times.* "Gossamer Silk from Spiders Spun." www.nytimes.com/2009/09/23/arts/design/23spiders.html?_r=3&pagewanted=1&tntemail1=y&emc=tnt

Small Stock Foods: www.smallstockfoods.com/index.php

Sphingidae of the United States: www.silkmoths.bizland.com/usatable.htm

Spiders: An Electronic Field Guide: www.bio.brandeis.edu/fieldbio/Spiders_Savransky_Suhd_Brondstatter/Pages/Home_Page_final.html

Wikimedia Commons: http://commons.wikimedia.org/wiki/Main_Page

World's Largest Saturniidae Site!: www.silkmoths.bizland.com/indexos.htm

Index

INDEX

INDEX